OSPREY/**AIRWAR** SERIES   EDITOR: MARTIN WINDROW

GERMAN FIGHTER UNITS
JUNE 1917-1918

BY ALEX IMRIE

COLOUR PLATES BY
MICHAEL ROFFE
TERRY HADLER
GERRY EMBLETON

OSPREY PUBLISHING LONDON

Published in 1978 by
Osprey Publishing Ltd
Member company of the George Philip Group
12–14 Long Acre, London WC2E 9LP
© Copyright 1978 Osprey Publishing Ltd

ISBN 0 85045 289 9

Some of the photographs used in this book and in *German
Fighter Units 1914–May 1917* originated with Messrs A. E.
Ferko, P. M. Grosz, W. R. Puglisi and B. J. Schmäling, to
whom the author extends his thanks.

Filmset by BAS Printers Limited, Over Wallop,
Hampshire, England
Printed in Hong Kong

ON THE DEFENSIVE

During the early part of 1917 most *Jagdstaffeln* were operating at half of their planned strengths due to problems in the supply of aircraft and pilots. *Kogenluft*, realizing that the supply situation would prevent the formation of a larger number of *Jagdstaffeln*, issued an order to increase the established strengths of the existing fighter units, as and when personnel and material became available.[1] It was also intended to considerably increase the size of the *Jagdstaffelschule* at Valenciennes. An increase in strength to fifty aeroplanes was planned, and to meet this requirement all D Category aircraft with their associated spare parts held by any *Armee Flug Park* were to be released to the *Jastaschule*. Additionally, all Albatros D III machines returned to Germany for major repair were not to be retained there for school use, as was the general rule for all other types due to the shortage of aircraft in Germany, but were to be returned to the front. It was not until the end of June that the supply situation improved sufficiently to enable unit strengths to approach the laid down establishments.

1. *Kogenluft* 62015/17 dated 1 May 1917 increased the establishment of *Jagdstaffeln*, as defined in *Feldflugchef* order 929/16 dated 31 August 1916, by four single-seater fighter aeroplanes, four engine fitters and four airframe riggers. (See *German Fighter Units 1914–May 1917*, Appendix I)

The increase in aerial activity during the summer demanded an increase in the number of fighter units, but *Kogenluft*, fearing a repetition of the supply problem, initially authorized the formation of only three new *Jagdstaffeln* for the Western Front when *Jasta* 39, 40, and 41 came into being and *Jagdstaffel* 38 was formed in Macedonia.

There were no direct entry fighter pilots at this time. All applicants to go on to single-seaters were required to hold the pilots' flying badge, which was only obtained after a number of operational flights. This experience was first obtained in the two-seater units, and although many of these formations eventually lost their best pilots to the *Jagdstaffeln*, this did not provide sufficient numbers.

The main Allied effort was transferred to the British front in Flanders during the early summer of 1917. The object of the fighting there, encompassed in the Battles of Ypres, was to clear the enemy from the Belgian coast and turn the flank of the German defence system. The brunt of these attacks fell on

New Albatros D Vs await collection at *Armee Flug Park* IV at Ghent. The high headrest fitted to these aircraft was often removed in service since it restricted rearward vision. The aircraft second from right (2005/17) was allocated to *Jagdstaffel* 12 and ferried to Epinoy on 2 July 1917 by the *Staffelführer*, *Oblt*. Adolf Ritter von Tutschek, whose permanent mount it became.

Leutnant **Werner Voss**, *Staffelführer Jagdstaffel* 10. Utterly fearless, Voss was one of Germany's most skilful fighter pilots. He brought down 50 enemy aeroplanes in under ten months before being killed in a single-handed combat against seven pilots from No. 56 Sqn. on 23 September 1917. He was then twenty years old.

German IV Army. The intensive use of Allied formations on this front could only be countered by ruthlessly robbing the other Army fronts of all possible *Jagdstaffeln* and transferring them to IV Army area. As a result there was a steady increase in the number of flying units allocated to this army until a total of sixteen *Jagdstaffeln* were poised in the area from the River Douve to the sea. These units were engaged in sporadic air fighting that mainly took place in the vicinity of Ypres–Roulers–Menin, both before and during the preliminary fighting that resulted in the Allies capturing the Messines Ridge.

The effective deployment of *Jagdstaffeln* within the organization of an army had not at this time really been established. At first, during late 1916 and early 1917, a central control via the *Armee Ober Kommando* (AOK) in a similar manner to that exercised over the KEK was favoured, since the aerial situation could best be judged from the AOK, a system favoured by the small number of units then in use. However, there was strong suggestion that the *Jagdstaffeln* allocated to an army should be divided amongst the *Gruppenkommandos* (Army Group HQs), since it was in their fighting areas that the tactical air-fighting zones lay. Owing to the intensive concentration of *Jagdstaffeln* in IV Army area, it became possible to allocate more than one unit each to the *Gruppenkommandos* and the collection and operation of these *Jasta* under one leader then became a necessity. However the leaders of these early groups of fighters seldom led them in the air, their temporary grouping at this time being merely an interim measure to be able to bring comparative numbers of fighters into contact with the large enemy formations that were now frequently appearing. Such assemblies of fighter units lacked cohesive methods of operation and positive leadership during combat, however, and it rapidly became obvious that better results would be obtained from the formation of permanent groups of *Jagdstaffeln* under active commanders well versed in the practice of leading fighting formations. These men would readily adapt to the extra responsibilities resulting from leading the combined strength of the group into battle. On 24 June the first moves were made to form such a permanent group when *Jagdstaffeln* 4, 6, 10, and 11 were fused into one formation designated *Jagdgeschwader* 1 and placed under the overall command of *Rittmeister* Manfred von Richthofen.

Even as the final stages of creating JG 1 were under way and before Richthofen had been able to lead his new *Jagdgeschwader* into action, he was wounded in aerial combat on 6 July, which forcibly removed him from the scene for six weeks. During his incapacitation Richthofen had time to reflect on the serious position that the German fighter force found itself in, and the sudden change that had come about in just over two short months since the successes in April. The use by the enemy of large formations and their introduction of improved single-seaters had robbed the Albatros D III of the superiority that it had previously enjoyed. The increase in losses that resulted and problems in the supply of replacement aircraft and pilots, which did not allow fighter units to operate for any protracted period at their full established strengths, were now causing a definite wane in the morale of the fighter pilots and had even affected the number of volunteers for such duties. The machine with which Richthofen's four component *Jagdstaffeln* were presently equipped was the Albatros D V, a type that Richthofen did not like. It was outclassed not only by the new Allied single-seaters but was also inferior to the new enemy fighting two-seaters. Richthofen felt that *Idflieg* were resting on their laurels, and that other aircraft manufacturing companies should be encouraged to challenge the apparent monopoly held by the Albatros *Flugzeugwerke*. He was especially interested in the new Fokker Triplane which was currently held up by the lack of rotary engines.

Before Richthofen was wounded he had had differences with *Kofl* 4, *Hauptmann* Otto Bufe, about the employment of the sixteen *Jagdstaffeln* then on the strength of IV Army. For some weeks the majority of these units had scored very few victories, a lack of success that did not reflect on the ability of the pilots or their individual *Staffelführer*, but on the strict orders of *Kofl* 4, who was a protagonist of the aerial barrage system of patrols. When *Jasta* 11 began to operate in IV Army area Bufe told Richthofen that he did not concern himself with victories, but that he wanted fighters at his disposal up on a strict time-table that defined place and height for the one and one quarter hours of useful fighter endurance. The very nature of this method of use was against the basic principles of operating *Jagdstaffeln*; fighters merely being used

to provide standing patrols had already been shown to be ineffective over twelve months previously during the Battle of Verdun. However, there were occasions when this system could produce results, especially if the *Luftschutzoffiziere* coverage or communication with these forward observers was incomplete, and there can be no doubt that there were strategic considerations in Bufe's handling of the situation that were not appreciated by Richthofen. Other *Staffelführer* of IV Army fighter units were unhappy with this restrictive order but were forced to abide by it, since they were directly under the orders of *Hptm.* Bufe. Richthofen was in some measure able to oppose Bufe and had from the outset not allowed *Jagdstaffel* 11 to be encumbered by this system of operation. The order did not apply to *Jagdgeschwader* 1 when it was formed, since that formation was directly under orders from IV Army HQ.

Previously Richthofen had not agreed with *Hptm.* Sorg, the *Kofl* of IV Army, when the first barrage flights were being planned for the use of combined *Jagdstaffeln* strengths for the first time towards the end of April. Richthofen had eventually had his way with Sorg and did not engage in many barrage patrols, although the initial use of fighters in strength on such duties really

Vizefeldwebel **Schleichardt of** *Jagdstaffel* **15 taking off from Boncourt aerodrome in his Albatros D V (2226/17), summer 1917. Despite the shortcomings of the Albatros D V, there were more of this type than any other machine at the front during the late summer and autumn of 1917.**

Albatros single-seaters of *Jagdstaffel* 12 on parade, Roucourt aerodrome near Douai, September 1917. All machines, including the unit two-seater hack (AEG C IV), carry the black tail unit signifying *Jasta* 12. Note the wide range of fuselage insignia for individual pilot identification.

formed the basis for the formation of *Jagdgeschwader* 1. Now in proportion to the numbers of enemy aircraft in IV Army area the numbers brought down were very small. During the Battle of Arras there had actually been fewer enemy aircraft present, but then their numbers had been grievously reduced by persistent attack. The day following Richthofen's wounding, *Jagdgeschwader* 1 under the command of *Oberleutnant* von Doering was able to score nine victories without loss, a sign that even without its famous leader's guiding hand, it was already an aggressive fighting force that would not hesitate to engage a numerically superior enemy whenever he dared to venture into German sky.

During this crisis period for the German fighter force, when technical difficulties affected aircraft supply and the shortage of suitably trained pilots produced serious gaps in *Jagdstaffeln* strengths, the declaration of war by the US presented an additional problem to *Kogenluft*. It was generally felt that the potential of American force was grossly exaggerated, but *Kogenluft* did not underestimate

the new threat, and seriously considered that American intervention in the conflict would soon become a major factor in the air war. Aviation support for the Allies from American sources could be expected by the end of 1917, with operational availability of US squadrons by early 1918. By then it was essential that German counter-measures should be complete. *Oberstleutnant* Thomsen, chief of the general staff of the *Luftstreitkräfte*, and *Major* Siegert of *Idflieg* already knew the only course open to them. They saw the *Jagdstaffeln* as a prerequisite to the continued successful operation of the army co-operation aeroplanes, and called for the urgent development of the fighting units. On 23 June 1917, *Kogenluft* put forward a plan, known as the *Amerikaprogramm*, to the OHL that called for a 100 per cent increase in the number of *Jagdstaffeln* by March 1918. Allied with this plan were various other changes to increase aircraft and aero-engine production, fuel and oil output and the manufacture of aircraft machine guns. To provide fighting instruction for the large numbers of new fighter pilots that would be required, it was necessary to form a second *Jagdstaffelschule*. A special objective of the *Amerikaprogramm* was the emphasis laid on the request to the aircraft industry to spare no effort in producing a new fighter aeroplane, technically superior to any machine that the Allies might bring out. To power this aircraft an absolute essential was

Leutnant Sachsenberg, *Staffelführer* of I *Marine-Feld-Jagdstaffel,* taking off in his Albatros D Va (5426/17) marked with a black and white diced fuselage band, while other machines of his unit follow suit. Aertrycke aerodrome, late summer 1917.

the evolution of a reliable high performance engine.

The factor that gave *Jagdgeschwader* 1 pilots a special advantage over the other *Jagdstaffeln* being operated in groups was the feeling of purpose and of belonging to the most élite fighter formation. They were highly competent and were continually inspired by the Boelcke spirit that Richthofen injected into the *Jagdgeschwader.* However, the selection of suitable personnel for JG 1 was only made by seriously reducing the fighting potential of other *Jagdstaffeln.* The unit also undertook constant readiness that led to concentrated operational flying: as a result, when formations were sent up from JG 1 it was not merely to mount patrols, but to engage enemy aircraft that had been reported by the forward *Luftschutzoffiziere.* In terms of air fighting, *Jasta* of JG 1 achieved far higher results in victory scores than did *Jagdstaffeln* assigned to the *Gruppenkommandos.* The reason why more *Jagdgeschwadern* were not formed immediately the effectiveness of JG 1 began to assert itself was because of the complete lack of suitable leaders. Regular officers with air fighting experience coupled with Richthofen's natural leadership qualities were just not available at the time and had to be nurtured. This was the reason given by *Kogenluft* and it reflects the cautious nature of Obstlt. Thomsen, the *Feldflugchef,* who, in order to ensure the continued success of such large permanent formations, had to

be satisfied that a properly qualified regular officer was in command. The *Jagdgeschwader* was held in reserve by the AOK and used as a rapid fighting instrument that could be unleashed in specially threatened areas of the army front to regain aerial superiority by attacking strong penetrations of enemy reconnaissance and bombing machines over the battle area and in the rear areas. The use of the *Jagdgeschwader* in this way ensured superiority in the upper air space. Much of the success was the direct result of Richthofen's continual drive to extract the finest in men and material for his formation. He had the ear of many superior officers in the right places, and if he needed anything he usually got it with the minimum of delay. He continually pressed for better aeroplanes and his component *Jagdstaffeln* were equipped with ever-improving types of aircraft.

The high losses experienced by the *Jagdstaffeln* during the summer of 1917, and the lack of sufficiently experienced two-seater pilots to train as fighter pilots, caused *Kogenluft* to relax the requirements in order to produce sufficient

7

Leutnant 'Papa' Güttler of Jasta Ober Ost in his LFG D II, Eastern Front, late 1917. Güttler's nickname stemmed from the fact that he was forty-four years of age, but he was still not the oldest German fighter pilot! In 1918 Güttler was Adjutant of Jagdstaffel 81, as Jasta Ober Ost became.

Leutnant Ernst Udet, Staffelführer of Jasta 37, looping his Albatros D Va over Metz. This machine is depicted in the colour plate on p. 30.

numbers of pilots for the new *Jasta* about to be formed. Suitable pupil pilots were able to go straight to the *Jagdstaffelschulen* from the flying schools. As a result pilots began to reach the *Jagdstaffeln* without the background of operational flying that their predecessors possessed. It was soon noted that this was a serious failing, and the general lack of knowledge, especially in aircraft recognition, soon made itself felt. Pilots attacked German aircraft by mistake and often mistook Allied machines as friendly and were as a result shot down. In an attempt to rectify this deficiency, captured Allied aircraft were made available at the *Jastaschulen*, where pilots could become familiar with them both on the ground and in the air. Many of the new units formed early in 1918 consisted of these direct entry fighter pilots. Where possible the units were released from frontline duties and based in rear areas, where air-firing, mock combat and formation flying were practised more intensively than had been done at the *Jastaschulen*. The most important aspect of this working up was that it was done in complete units under the *Staffelführer* who would later take the unit into action.

More attention was now focused on the temporary grouping of *Jagdstaffeln* and on 28 October the first five of twelve *Führer der Jagdgruppen (Gruja)* were made permanent establishments. Although the component *Jagdstaffeln* and the number of units within a *Jagdgruppe* still changed depending on the tactical situation, there was less change than hitherto, and the improved cohesion resulted in more effective operational use. The use of the *Jagdgruppen* took place over fighting areas that were designated *Jagdraüme*, the limits of which were generally in agreement with the battle areas of the *Gruppenkommandos*. It was the responsibility of the *Jagdgruppe* to safeguard and protect the army co-operation working aeroplanes engaged upon artillery observation and reconnaissance: the aerial combats that they became involved in were really only a means to this end.

Good though the bulk of the *Jagdstaffeln* were, they were still usually well below their full establishment. Units that did on occasion reach full strength were seldom able to maintain this serviceability state due to the high attrition rate of aircraft that could not be kept pace with by the poor supply of replacement machines—adequate proof that the *Jagdstaffel* programme from the autumn of 1916 had overestimated the strength and quantity production from factories in Germany. Before the first forty *Jagdstaffeln* were up to full fighting strength with sufficient reserves to cater for the high attrition rate being experienced, the *Amerika-programm* demanded the formation of a further forty *Jagdstaffeln*. That these units, produced at such short notice under the constant demand for every available aeroplane of the D Category, would never be completely up to strength was a strong possibility fully appreciated by *Kogenluft*.

The planned output from the moves made under the *Amerikaprogramm* was never completely met, despite the utmost effort by the German aircraft industry, which included modernization of old factories, introduction of new companies, and the foundation of special repair workshops. Instead of a required output of 2,500 aero-engines a month, only 1,400 a month were being delivered by 1 March 1918, although this figure rose to 1,600 per month by June. Equally, only 1,800 aeroplanes were being delivered each month instead of 2,000. These failings made it impossible to completely equip the *Jagdstaffeln* to the planned strengths of eighteen aircraft each. In addition the calculated requirement on aviation fuel was not completely assured. In January 1918 the monthly fuel delivery was 6,000 tons, only 50 per cent of the amount required by 1 March, and although the *Jagdstaffeln* were operating at most with only two-thirds of their planned fighting strengths during March, a system of fuel rationing had to be introduced.

Following the successes of JG 1, two further such formations emerged on 2 February 1918 when *Jagdstaffeln* 12, 13, 15, and 19 under the overall command of *Hptm.* Adolf Ritter von Tutschek became *Jagdgeschwader* 2; and *Jagdstaffeln Boelcke*, 26, 27, and 36 under *Hptm.* Bruno Loerzer comprised *Jagdgeschwader* 3.

Leutnant **Gontermann** *Staffelführer* of *Jasta* **15, taking off in Fokker Dr I 115/17 from Boncourt aerodrome on 30 October 1917. Gontermann died from injuries received on this flight when he crashed due to structural failure of the upper wing.**

Oberleutnant **Bodenschatz**, *Adjutant* of *Jagdgeschwader* **1, in front of a Fokker Dr I during the winter of 1917/1918. This officer served throughout the war in this capacity under the three JG 1** *Kommandeure*, **Richthofen, Reinhard and Göring. He rose to high rank in the Luftwaffe and still attends the yearly traditional meetings of** *Jagdgeschwader Freiherr von Richthofen Nr 1.*

OFFENSIVE IN THE WEST

During the spring of 1918 the German fighter force stood at the very pinnacle of its power as regards material and numerical strength and despite the shortcomings of the *Amerikaprogramm* the OHL had 80 *Jasta* at their disposal. It was decided to attack on the general line Arras–La Fère to obtain a decision in favour of the Central Powers by means of a massive breakthrough in the direction of Amiens before fresh American resources could be introduced into the final struggle. With II, XVII, and XVIII German Armies having concentrated their strengths in their rear areas from the beginning of March, the day of attack was determined as 21 March: XVII and XVIII Armies were to be introduced on either side of II Army which was already in position. On the day of

commencement of the battle, the three attack armies had an allocation of 35 *Jagdstaffeln*, a number which was to increase further during the battle until more than 50 per cent of all the *Jagdstaffeln* were engaged in the fighting. The success of the German attack depended on surprise. In previous large-scale battles the offensive intentions of the Allies had in part been given away on certain sectors of the front by the increase in aerial activity and the appearance of new aerodromes. The Germans spared no effort to prevent this happening on this occasion. Great care was taken in increasing the number of flying units, not only within the attack armies but also in the neighbouring army areas. Increased *Jagdstaffel* activity was forbidden, and pilots from *Jagdstaffeln* located on other fronts who would eventually be engaged in the fighting were attached to *Jasta* in the attack area from the end of February for area familiarization. Hangars were not allowed to be erected, portable tent hangars were to be pitched first only on the evening of the first day of battle, and the occupation of new operational aerodromes was not made until the evening before the attack. To

One of the few German single-seater fighters to be started by hand-swinging the propeller was the Fokker Dr I triplane. Here *Ltn.* Steinhäuser tries his hand at starting the Oberursel rotary for a fellow pilot. *Jagdstaffel 11*, Cappy aerodrome, March 1918.

Warming up OAW-built Albatros D III of *Jasta* 57. Even with the advent of better single-seaters, the Albatros D III did not disappear from front line units, and 357 machines of this type were recorded at the front at the end of February 1918.

help in the dissemination of forces, some units had their aircraft stored in a dismantled condition in farm buildings throughout the area and in neighbouring army areas, and these machines were only assembled shortly before the attack was due to begin. When *Jagdstaffeln* did arrive in the area they occupied existing aerodromes, and were only used to support units that had already been based for some time in the attack area as long as there was no danger of them being recognized, which would have given the enemy some indication of the concentration taking place.

The fighter utilization planned for XVIII Army for 21 March was to commence at 0600 hrs, when the *Jagdstaffeln* would attack all enemy aircraft and thus allow the army co-operation aircraft full protection. They were also to prevent the entry of Allied reconnaissance machines into the area. *Jagdgeschwader* 2 would fight in the upper airspace and so protect the low flying fighters, and also secure aerial superiority on the left flank of the army, supported by *Jagdstaffeln* from VII Army. From 0700 hrs, aircraft of JG 2 and other *Jagdstaffeln* directly under *Kofl* orders would concentrate their attacks on the enemy observation balloons. By means of continuous attack they were to destroy the balloons or ensure that they did not ascend. The *Kofl* expected that from 0800 hrs he would have

sufficient fighter resources available to enable them to counter the expected increase in enemy aerial activity that a successful infantry breakthrough would bring. It was essential that all fighter aircraft were to be refuelled and rearmed to immediate readiness as soon as possible after their return from their initial sorties. *Jagdgeschwader* 2 and *Rittmeister* von Braun, the *Führer* of *Jagdgruppe* 5, were to keep the *Kofl* continuously advised on the strength and readiness states of their component *Jagdstaffeln*.

Fighter Units and Bases 21 March 1918
XVII Army

Jagdgeschwader 3 (*Jasta Boelcke*, 26, 27, & 36)	Erchin
Jagdstaffel 14	Masny
Jagdstaffel 20	Guesnain
Jagdstaffel 23	Aniche
Jagdstaffel 32	Guesnain
Jagdstaffel 35	Emerchicourt
Jagdstaffel 40	Masny
Jagdstaffel 49	Bruille les Marchiennes
Jagdstaffel 58	Emerchicourt
Jagdstaffel 59	Emerchicourt

II Army

Jagdgeschwader 1 (Jasta 4 & 6)	Lieu/St Amand
(Jasta 10 & 11)	Avesnes le Sec
Jagdstaffel 5	Libramont
Jagdstaffel 16	Le Cateau
Jagdstaffel 37	Le Cateau
Jagdstaffel 46	Bevillers
Jagdstaffel 54	Neuvilly
Jagdstaffel 56	Neuvilly

XVIII Army

Jagdgeschwader 2 (Jasta 12, 13, 15, & 19)	Ch Balâtre
Jagdstaffel 8	Wassigny
Jagdstaffel 22	La Ferté Fe
Jagdstaffel 24	Guise
Jagdstaffel 44	Pleine Selve
Jagdstaffel 48	Guise
Jagdstaffel 53	Mont d'Origny
Jagdstaffel 69	Origny/St Bénois
Jagdstaffel 79	Villers le Sec

XVII ARMY

Bad weather with low cloud prevented many of the planned activities until nearly midday on 21 March. The concentration of the *Jasta* secured aerial supremacy and allowed the work of the army co-operation aircraft to be carried out without interference. Confrontation with enemy forces in the air, due to the surprise attack and the bad weather, was very weak and no enemy squadron crossed the lines. From midday on 22 March an increase in enemy aerial activity was noticed. This was marked against XVII Army front, where it was expected that the enemy would make a determined attempt to hold Arras. In the afternoon *Jagdgeschwader* 3 was engaged in a fierce air battle with enemy squadrons over the Cambrai area and succeeded in breaking up the enemy formations forcing their withdrawal behind their own lines. On 23 March the focal point of enemy opposition, interfering with the army co-operation aircraft, lay in the vicinity of Beugny some 6 kilometres east of Bapaume. Continuous attacks by *Jagdgeschwader* 3 and the other *Jagdstaffeln* made it possible to force the numerically superior enemy formations back and to shoot down twelve enemy aeroplanes. Low-level activity was, however, not so successful and enemy aircraft engaging in the ground fighting were seen for the first time. On 24 and 25 March, because of good weather and a continually strengthening enemy, a difficult situation was presented to the *Jagdstaffeln*. The main combat area on 25 March was over Bapaume; strong British squadrons, operating in continuous waves, considerably interfered with the work of the *Jagdstaffeln*, and it was not possible to prevent enemy aircraft penetration. A heavy bombing raid by *Bogohl* 5 on Doullens aerodrome is thought to have been a contributory factor in the decrease in enemy aerial activity on 27 March. Formations of up to sixty-strong enemy aircraft were seen during the morning of 26 March, but a day later only small formations were encountered.

II ARMY

Bad weather was also the reason that fighter units were not in action before 1300 hrs on 21 March; however the *Jagdstaffeln* carried out their assigned duties and provided complete protection for the army co-operation aircraft. *Jagdgeschwader* 1, working at heights between 5,500 and 6,000 metres, prevented the breakthrough of enemy squadrons. In the lower levels, *Jagdstaffeln* attacked enemy

fighters and reconnaissance squadrons, although activity was not great until 1600 hrs, when a sudden upsurge took place: particularly strong enemy formations appeared over Havrincourt Wood and were engaged and forced to retire behind their own lines. Poor weather on 22 March again prevented flying operations before midday, but enemy opposition was not great and British aircraft were first seen at 1500 hrs. They were immediately attacked and forced to retire. Some enemy formations were able to effect penetration and drop bombs in the forward area, but generally the *Jagdstaffeln* enjoyed aerial superiority. More activity came on 23 March with an improvement in the weather, enemy bombers attacking Cambrai and Sailly. At midday on 24 March the enemy put up strong standing patrols at all levels and repeated them in the evening. Strengthened enemy aerial opposition with standing patrols at all levels on 25 and 26 March made things more difficult for the numerically inferior *Jagdstaffeln*, and this enemy activity increased even more on 27 March, especially over Albert. However a decrease was noticed in the afternoon after *Jagdgeschwader* 1 had operated several sweeps around Albert. In general the *Jagdstaffeln* had a more difficult time because of the numerically superior enemy squadrons. Low cloud and fog on the German side of the line reduced the *Jagdstaffeln* activity on 28 March, but the enemy participation was particularly strong.

XVIII ARMY

It was the same story in this area on 21 March, and no flying was carried out until midday due to bad weather. Enemy activity was light in the morning but increased in the afternoon. That the *Jagdstaffeln* possessed aerial superiority was still apparent on 22 March when, from 1300 hrs, escorts were provided for infantry aeroplanes flying at 500 metres to determine the extent of the advance. There was much activity on 23 March and support for the British came in the form of strong French squadrons, which attacked from the south. The numerical inferiority of the *Jagdstaffeln* and the better performance in speed and rate of climb of the enemy aircraft made itself felt. The continuous operation of the German fighters enabled a large number of successful combats to take place, but the *Jagdstaffeln* just could not prevent the army co-operation machines being interfered with by enemy fighters. On 24 March there was strong aerial activity, and in continuous fighting the *Jagdstaffeln* were able to force the withdrawal of the enemy formations to behind their own lines. Despite his overwhelming numerical superiority, there were generally no breakthroughs made by the enemy, and he was compelled to operate mostly over or behind his own lines. The greatest activity encountered since the battle commenced took place on 25 and 26 March, when enemy machines joined in the ground fighting. German fighters had a difficult task in balancing the effect of enemy activity but finally, on 27 March, poor weather generally reduced the scale of fighting in the air and brought some respite for the hard-working *Jagdstaffeln*.

Panoramic view of Lechelle taken a few hours after *Jagdgeschwader* 1 occupied the aerodrome during the advance, 26 March 1918. Fokker Dr I triplanes of *Jasta* 6 and 10 are lined up while mechanics refuel and rearm them. The observer, keeping a watch for enemy aircraft, is using tripod-mounted binoculars, while on his right in the background can be seen the deck-chairs for pilots on immediate readiness.

Mechanics of *Jasta* 13 digging 1·5m deep slit-trenches between the barrack huts on Balâtre aerodrome near Roye. These trenches were put to good use on the night of 12/13 April 1918, when a bombardment caused 200 high explosive shells to fall on the aerodrome destroying 25 aeroplanes of *Jagdgeschwader* 2.

FRONT LINE AIRFIELDS

Although once again a ruthless denuding of other fronts of their *Jagdstaffeln* took place it was impossible to allocate each *Gruppenkommando* with the same strength of fighters as had been done during the fighting in Flanders. Also, because the focal point of the ground and aerial situation could not be foreseen it was impossible to assign specific strengths of fighters to certain *Gruppenkommandos*. The fighter forces were centrally located and allocated special fighting areas and were controlled from the AOK. Generally the employment of the fighters was as had been experienced in Flanders, although once again the patrol flights that were undertaken because of the nature of the tactical use of the *Jagdstaffeln* were criticized. The concealment of the concentration before the attack proved to have been a success, and although the enemy may have expected an attack, he was unable to determine the sector of the front on which it would take place. Accounts vary as to the effectiveness of the wireless telegraphy links between the *Jagdstaffeln* and their forward *Luftschutzoffiziere*: some units reported excellent results while others complained that the isolated messages were insufficient for the tactical requirement of bringing the *Jagdstaffeln* into action. Some *Gruppenkom-*

mandos undertook to make their *Luftschutzoffiziere* mobile for the advance, with the result that contact with them was soon lost. The part of XVIII Army's fighter force that expected to make a considerable rapid advance moved its forward aerodromes as near as possible to the front line, in order to control its own operation, having lost contact with its forward observers. In several instances these aerodromes came under heavy enemy artillery fire and the *Jagdstaffeln* concerned were compelled to retire, causing unnecessary complication in their aerial operations.

Moving the fighter aerodromes forward generally presented very great difficulties during the advance: the whole area west of the original German front line was unsuitable for aerodromes of any kind. *Jagdgeschwadern* and *Jagdstaffeln* were allocated special aerodromes, in the main enemy aerodromes, which were occupied on the third day of the advance. British personnel had, however, destroyed all hangars and equipment, and only small amounts of fuel and rubber were captured. Although these aerodromes were located at maximum range for the enemy artillery, because of the unavoidable concentration of aircraft upon them, they were inviting targets, but despite many bombing attacks the losses due to this cause were very small. Moving equipment and stores forward across the shelled area was accomplished by collecting all the available lorries on the strength of the *Jasta*, but shortages of transport soon became apparent, which in turn weakened the readiness of some *Jagdstaffeln*. The cost in material and personnel during the battle had been enormous. However, it was just possible to maintain the strengths of the flying units by means of the well-organized supply system up to 28 March. The forward locations of storage depots for aviation fuel was a factor that greatly helped in this matter. The success in the air fighting between 21 and 28 March was ensured by the concentrated assembly of the *Jagdstaffeln*. Placing the *Jagdgeschwadern* under the control of the AOK was also proven to have been correct. These permanent formations fought the enemy over the whole army area, the remaining *Jagdstaffeln* coming under the orders of the *Grufl*, who then allocated them one or more army group sectors as their fighting areas. The fighting zone of the *Jagdgeschwader* extended over the borders of the AOK area and those of the *Jagdgruppen* over the borders of the *Gruppenkommandos*. This method was generally the rule during the battle and was also used until the end of the war, although the battle situation, position of aerodromes, communication effectiveness and the views of the individual *Kofl* frequently caused divergencies from this basic allocation of forces. The actual method of use during the battle was subject to continual change, and quick adaption to the given conditions was the real reason for the success.

When the successes of both German and Allied fighters are compared for the first eight days of the battle, it must be recognized that neither side held mastery of the air and neither could continually hold aerial superiority. Experience shows that the attacker, through the concentration of his fighter forces, held a superiority over the surprised enemy in the first days of the attack, but after a certain period of fighting, a balance was reached. Then, depending on the employment of forces and the battle situation, first one and then the other secured aerial superiority. The longer the operation lasted, the more certain the balance of the fighter forces became. It is considered that on 23 March the fighting was even; from 24 March, however, the numerical superiority of the enemy was the deciding factor, and this was only balanced by the high standard of devotion to duty and the prowess shown by the German fighter pilots. Inferior aircraft, numerical inferiority and incomplete reserves of personnel are the main reasons why the German air fighters could not always completely carry out the tasks assigned to them. As far as the strengths allowed, it was arranged that in the main days of the battle the continual occupation of the airspace over the fighting area was achieved. Had the fighting been quieter a roster for morning, midday and evening sorties for some of the *Jagdstaffeln* could have been introduced, in order that the other units could have rested, rearmed and refuelled at these times.

A necessary requirement to the success of the spring offensive was the careful selection of *Luftschutzoffiziere* who were experienced, and capable of making correct assessments of the situation, added to which was the need for a sound knowledge of aerial tactics of both sides, allied to a good understanding of all types of aircraft. As the aeroplanes of the *Jagdstaffeln* were inferior to those of the enemy, the Germans were in the unenviable position of awaiting attack from above to be able to

Mechanics of *Jasta* 26 assist pilots with flying kit before they undertake a patrol in their Fokker Dr I triplanes. Erchin aerodrome, April 1918.

Jagdstaffel 73 Pfalz Dr I triplane on Mars sous Bourcq aerodrome. Although many companies produced triplane prototypes, the Fokker and Pfalz triplanes were the only ones to reach the front. There were 180 triplanes at the front at the end of April 1918 and only 9 of these were Pfalz machines.

fight at all, as they simply could not reach the high flying enemy formations. Both the Pfalz D IIIa and Albatros D Va could only climb to approximately 4,500 metres and neither type was fast enough or possessed sufficient manoeuvrability. The Fokker Dr I could reach 6,000 metres, but it too was not fast enough. Nevertheless the armament of these machines was equal to that of enemy aircraft: all types were fitted with two machine guns synchronized to fire through the arc swept by the revolving propeller and carried 1,000 rounds of ammunition.

That the German air fighting force found itself in a crisis at the end of March 1918 was reflected in a report written by von Richthofen himself, shortly before his death on 21 April 1918. Based on his experiences of leading large fighting formations, von Richthofen's report included the following extract, which highlights the performance handicap under which the German fighters were operated in the spring of 1918:

During periods of very intensive aerial activity one is forced to work with formations composed of from 30 to 40 machines. The reason for this is the inferiority of the German fighter aeroplane and the frequent use by the enemy of strong squadron strengths. The formation to be adopted when operating such groups is to have a *Staffel* to the right and left of the *Kommandeur* and slightly

Mechanics prepare a striped fuselage Pfalz D IIIa of *Jasta* 30 for flight, April 1918. The unit marking, a black bordered orange diamond, can be seen on the side of the fuselage near the cockpit.

behind him, while the other two *Staffeln* are located directly behind the *Kommandeur*, one following the other but flying 100 metres higher than the leader. The object of operating such a formation up is to destroy enemy squadrons; attacks on single enemy aeroplanes are pointless. For this reason it is only worthwhile to put such formations up during good weather when considerable enemy aerial activity is expected. The most advantageous use is when one can position oneself between the front lines and an enemy squadron that has achieved penetration. His return route has been cut: climb above him and force him to fight. The formation attack leads to success. When the *Kommandeur* has decided to attack, he flies towards the main part of the enemy squadron. Shortly before he attacks, he slows

Short back and sides! A member of *Jasta* 19 allows the barber to apply his skill at Nesle in April 1918 with a backcloth of unit motor transport.

down so that the rest of the *Geschwader*, which may have become dispersed because of manoeuvring, can regain its original formation. Each individual pilot counts the number of machines in the enemy squadron from the time that he first sees it. At the moment when the attack commences every pilot must know the exact whereabouts of all the enemy aeroplanes, and at the very instant that the *Kommandeur* makes his dive at the enemy formation, it must be the aim of every single pilot to be the first to come to grips with the enemy. The concentration of the first attack, brought about by the determination of each pilot to join combat, will break up the enemy formation. Once this happens the shooting down of the enemy is then only a case of single combats. There is an ever-present danger that pilots will be impeded by the close proximity to one another during the fight, and possibly because of this concern, give some of the enemy a chance of escaping. It must therefore be an absolute rule that only the pilot who is closest to the enemy machine shoots at it. It is completely wrong for several pilots to become involved with one enemy aircraft and follow it down while so engaged. Following such a *Geschwader* attack when it successfully breaks up the enemy formation and the *Geschwader* into single combats, it is not easy for the *Kommandeur* to assemble his forces again. He should circle over the main fighting area, or over a previously determined landmark; single pilots will then formate on him and if the formation assumes sufficient strength the fighting patrol can be resumed. Sometimes it is not possible to climb above a very high flying enemy formation. When this happens one has to remain with the *Geschwader* in the vicinity of the front lines at a position where one estimates the enemy formation will cross the front on its return. When

the enemy squadron appears, one flies along underneath it and tries to entice the enemy to join combat by using dive and zoom tactics, or by making steep full throttle climbs in his direction. Very often this has the desired effect, and especially the British normally accept the challenge. An enemy aircraft usually dives on a single German machine, mostly the last aircraft in the formation, and then climbs again. When an aircraft is attacked in this way, the pilot can best counter the attack by turning with full throttle, while the remainder of the *Geschwader* tries to climb above the attacker. It is usually possible that single machines of the *Geschwader* will in this way get to the same height as the attacking aircraft, then by gaining height during turning, get above the enemy machine and shoot it down. Such fights can often take minutes to carry out, and during this time the *Kommandeur* must continually circle. As a result of this manoeuvring the *Geschwader* loses its standard formation, and no attempt should be made to regain formation. Instead all pilots must close up on the *Kommandeur* and try to gain height while turning with him. Straight and level flight at this time is dangerous, since the enemy formation is waiting for just such an opportunity to dive unnoticed out of the sun. Practice flights in *Geschwader* strength are not necessary when each individual *Staffel* is well practised and is capable of formation flying.

Leutnant Loewenhardt, the *Staffelführer* of *Jagdstaffel* 10, had engaged in several successful attacks against observation balloons, and had brought down four in the first three months of 1918 while flying Albatros D Va and Pfalz D IIIa aircraft. He had this to say about his methods, which he considered under two headings:

1 Alone. Dusk is the best time for a balloon attack. Low-level flight is made to the front, and a note made of the position and height of the balloon, which is usually situated some 6 kilometres behind the front line. After sunset, climb to 3,000 or 4,000 metres depending on the wind, fly back to the front and glide towards the balloon when this can be reached in a steep glide. The enemy cannot then hear the attacker. [Loewenhardt had never been fired at by enemy anti-aircraft fire before any of his attacks commenced.] Attack with machine-gun fire at a range not greater than 50 metres. A short burst will set the balloon on fire. When flying home in the dark, climb steeply, since the British anti-aircraft defences believe that the attacker will dive away, and as a result they fire too low. A solo attack during the day is impossible. When the sky is completely overcast one can easily be surprised by enemy aircraft; the balloons are difficult to find since the approach must be made either in or above the clouds. The balloons are usually flown 300 to 400 metres under the cloud base; as a result it is not possible to climb quickly into the clouds after the attack. Cumulus clouds

Local inhabitants show a keen interest in *Jagdstaffel Boelcke* Fokker Dr I triplanes on the aerodrome at Erchin north of Cambrai, April 1918.

at the same height as the balloon at a distance of from 2,000 to 3,000 metres are on occasion very useful.

2 Staffel *Attack*. The best time for this is either in the early morning or in the evening. Use as many aircraft as there are balloons to be attacked. Whoever arrives first at the balloon shoots first; repeat the attack until the balloon burns. During these repeat attacks, where possible fire at the same part of the balloon. The determination of each pilot to be the first at his balloon, ensures that the *Staffel* arrives in a group and this makes defence against enemy aircraft easier. Anti-aircraft guns fire at each aircraft and shared anti-aircraft fire is half anti-aircraft fire. Cumulus clouds are useful for balloon attacks in *Staffel* strength. The leader of the formation must keep a good look out for enemy aircraft. Attacks when the sky is completely overcast are not worthwhile since the *Staffel* never arrives at the balloons in any sort of concentration. Single pilots lose themselves in the clouds, and can easily be surprised by enemy aircraft. The ratio of machines used to losses experienced is not in keeping with the success rate and pilots lose confidence in the undertaking. The phosphorous ammunition used always promises success. An old balloon which has been aloft for a long time during the day, burns immediately. Wet and new balloons are not so easily set alight. [Loewenhardt loaded his ammunition belts for both guns where every fourth round was one of *Ph-Munition*.] It is basically wrong to undertake balloon attacks at specified times: it is equally wrong to order these attacks in this way. Our own fighter aeroplanes are inferior to those of the enemy; as a result the *Staffelführer* must wait for the best moment to make the attack; if there is no such correct opportunity, the attack should not be undertaken, and all aircraft should return to base.

BACKS TO THE WALL

The advance on II, XVII and XVIII Army fronts came to an end on 28 March. The plan of the OHL to divide the British and French armies had failed, although there were two further attacks against the British front, one at Armentières on 9 April and the second at Kemmel Hill on 25 April. In May and June two attacks were carried out against the French, at Soissons-Rheims on 27 May and between Montdidier and Noyon on 9 June, but the period between April and June 1918 covers the last successes of the German armies, and the turning point represents the beginning of a continued inferiority of the German Air Service due to the shortage of material and personnel.

Pilot losses in the German fighter units had been less than those experienced by the enemy, but they were more telling due to the numerical superiority of the Allied squadrons. The Fokker Dr I triplane had performed well during the offensive since it had mostly been used at low level owing to the low cloud, and some sorties of two hours duration had been spent at heights between 50 and 700 metres.

Attrition of aircraft had been very high, especially in *Jagdgeschwader* 1, due to forced landings made in the shelled area of the Somme after air fights. Richthofen kept pressing for better aeroplanes and wanted the new Fokker D VII—fitted if possible with the BMW engine—in sufficient numbers to completely equip a *Jasta*, but production was slow and he had to carry on operating his four component *Jagdstaffeln* equipped with machines greatly inferior to those of the enemy.

The following fighter units were assembled in VI Army area on 9 April for the attack on Armentières:

Jagdgruppe Nord (3) *Jasta* 40, 47, 49, 57, and 58
Jagdgruppe Süd (7b) *Jasta* 29, 30, 41, 43, and 52
Additional *Jasta* from XVII Army: *Jasta* 14, 18, 20, and 37.

The employment of these fighters was made very difficult because of bad weather and low cloud coupled with a lack of information from the battle area. This last difficulty arose because communication with the *Luftschutzoffiziere* via wireless telegraphy only provided for the most important type of messages. A fuller system of communication with telephone links had not been organized because of shortage of time. Since contact with these forward observers was insufficient and was on many occasions non-existent, information about the aerial situation was mainly obtained from returning aircraft and the troops themselves. These two sources were often at variance with each other and generally the information came too late to be acted upon.

Owing to the poor weather conditions, the main duty of the *Jagdstaffeln* lay in fighting low flying enemy aircraft and giving whatever protection was possible to the German infantry co-operation aeroplanes. The morale booster given to the German infantry by the constant aerial activity of the *Jagdstaffeln* was considerable. Flying in any sort of formation was impossible; aircraft lost their way, and pilots saw enemy machines first at very close range. During the first days of the battle, British aircraft engaged in the ground fighting gave the *Jasta* a completely new and extremely difficult task. Freedom of manoeuvre above heights of 400 metres was almost completely ruled out because of the cloud base. The British utilized this cloud cover to their advantage and their well-handled aeroplanes

attacking the German troops had a relatively easy task. They dived out of the cloud and approaching their targets almost unobserved, dropped their bombs and fired their machine guns before zooming into the cloud to avoid interception. Even in conditions of good visibility aircraft of the *Jagdstaffeln* would have had a difficult job to stop the enemy intruders, but in the prevailing conditions it was impossible. Contact with enemy aircraft was made only very occasionally, and the basic air fighting principle of the carefully planned attack resulting in surprise was impossible due to the sudden confrontation between aircraft. Another factor that did not help the hard-pressed German fighters was the better speed and rate of climb of the enemy machines. This situation, together with the desperate pleas of the fighting troops, and the fact

Unteroffizier **Moosbacher**, *Jagdstaffel* **77b, joins his mechanics in counting the holes in his Albatros D Va after having been subjected to particularly heavy anti-aircraft fire. Note that the change from Iron Cross to** *Balkenkreuz* **national insignia, ordered on 17 March 1918, has not yet been fully actioned on this machine.**

that additional machine gun distribution for anti-aircraft purposes did not seem to alter the situation at all (on 9 and 10 April only three enemy aircraft were brought down by machine gun fire from the ground) led to the AOK ordering two-thirds of all the *Jagdstaffeln* to be employed against the low flying British aircraft engaging in the ground fighting. The remaining one-third of the German fighters in VI Army (four *Jagdstaffeln*) were retained by the AOK to carry out what had been seen as the main fighter task—the protection of the German army co-operation aircraft in the area in front of the enemy infantry lines.

To enable them to carry out this AOK order, which was the only correct procedure to adopt to secure quicker effective use of the fighter force, it was decided to put *Jagdstaffeln* at readiness on advanced landing grounds and employ them from ground observation reports. The success of this move was immediate. From 13 April onwards the continual hinderance to the fighting troops was reduced and their complaints ceased. Both duties, protection of the army co-operation aeroplanes and the protection of the fighting troops, were well catered for. In general the success of the German fighter force, operating under the most difficult conditions, was undisputed. Apart from a few hours on 12 April during which the enemy carried out a concentrated surprise attack during a sudden weather improvement, the freedom of the air over and in front of the fighting area stayed with the German side during the entire battle.

The following fighter units were assembled in IV Army area on 25 April for the attack on the River Lys which resulted in the capture of Kemmel Hill:

> *Jagdgeschwader* 3 (*Jasta Boelcke*, 26, 27, and 36)
> *Jagdgruppe* 6 (*Jasta* 7, 16, 28, and 51)
> *Jagdgruppe* 10 (*Jasta* 20, 33, 40, 49, 57, and 58)
> *Jagdgruppe* 9 (*Jasta* 3, 54, and 56).

On the morning of 25 April at the same time as the infantry went over the top, sixteen *Schlachtstaffeln* attacked the villages of Kemmel, Kemmel Hill and Dranoutre. As the *Schlasta* were beginning their work, a strong force of fighters appeared over the battle area led by *Oblt.* Loerzer, the *Kommandeur* of *Jagdgeschwader* 3. This force comprised fourteen *Jagdstaffeln* (JG 3, *Jagdgruppen* 6 and 10), while the right flank was covered by *Jagdgruppe* 9, and on the left flank all *Jasta* from VI Army operated in tune with the Kemmel operation. The enemy, opposed by this massive aerial armada, was completely powerless. During the first day of the Kemmel battle one could speak exceptionally about an absolute German mastery of the air. This applied not only to the battle zone, but also extended far behind the enemy lines. Serious attempts to engage the German formations did not materialize and not one German aeroplane was shot down, either in aerial fighting or from the ground. The second German attack on 29 April, to enlarge on the successes achieved, met with stubborn resistance and the battle ceased on 1 May. Despite this attack's lack of success the *Jagdstaffeln* successfully carried out all the tasks allotted to them. Although at the beginning of May there was a pause in the ground fighting, there was no rest for the flying units. From the beginning of the month enemy aerial activity increased equally along the whole front from the Channel coast to the River Oise. The failure of the Allied fighters to successfully combat the *Jagdstaffeln* in the previous battles, the heavy losses that they had sustained (232 aeroplanes and 16 balloons in April) and possibly the importance of being able to recognize the place and time for the next German attack at any cost, may have been the reason for the sudden considerable increase in enemy aerial activity. Bombing and reconnaissance formations made continual penetration between the Rivers Scarpe and Oise, and enemy fighters flew patrols at all heights up to 6,000 metres. The *Jagdstaffeln* never ceased to join combat with the enemy squadrons

Three NCO pilots of *Jagdstaffel* 5. Left to right: *Vizefeldwebel* Rumey, Könnecke and Mai. By the end of May 1918, when this photograph was taken, their combined effort amounted to 50 aerial victories. This figure had increased to 110 by the end of the war: (Rumey 45, Könnecke 35 and Mai 30).

The oily-fingered brethren! Mechanics of *Jasta* 10 pose in front of one of the first Fokker D VIIs to reach the unit. The group includes: *Sergeant* **Jung**, *Unteroffiziere* **Grünewald**, **Lippmann, Chorus, Junginger** and **Rüser**, *Gefreiter* **Timm**, *Flieger* **Mandow, Klingenberg, Rehbohm, Schmidt, Wittke, Grabitz** and **Reihmann**.

and offered them strong resistance.

At the beginning of May the first large numbers of Fokker D VIIs reached the front. This aircraft was as good as the enemy's best: it was fast, had an excellent rate of climb and was highly manoeuvrable. The arrival of the D VII gave the *Jasta* pilots a new lease of life; their old confidence returned and as a direct result their successes increased. On the northern half of the British front the protection of army co-operation machines was assured and enemy squadron penetrations were, for the most part, effectively engaged. However, between Arras and Chauny the enemy could only be kept in check with difficulty, using all available *Jagdstaffeln*. The fierce fighting in this area resulted in a large number of victories. Due to the massive employment of numerically superior enemy forces the *Jagdstaffeln* had a most difficult task over the whole active front during the second half of May. The majority of the *Jagdstaffeln* were assembled in the threatened area of the Amiens bulge, and the remainder of the British front was comparatively weakly held. As a result enemy penetrations could not be prevented all the time. In concentrated attacks against these enemy squadrons some combats were fought successfully, and the number of Allied aircraft brought down during the month is proof of this activity (362 aeroplanes and 24 balloons in May). Because of the obvious concentration of both British and French forces on the British front, the OHL decided not to attack there but to make a surprise thrust against the French that would cause the removal of reserves from the British front and possibly make the resumption of an attack later against the British more feasible. Poised in VII Army area on 27 May for the battle of Chemin des Dames were the following fighter units:

Jagdgeschwader 1 (*Jasta* 4, 6, 10, and 11)
Jagdgeschwader 3 (*Jasta Boelcke*, 26, 27, and 36)
Jagdgruppe 5 (*Jasta* 22, 50, 63, 66, and 81).

By careful preparation and security, the breakthrough on VII Army front on 27 May was complete, and in continuous advance the River Marne near Chateau Thierry was reached on 31 May. On the ground and in the air the massive strength of VII Army completely surprised the enemy. From 27 to 30 May aerial superiority was with the *Jagdstaffeln*, enemy opposition being so weak in the upper levels that aircraft of all formations had plenty of opportunity to seek targets on the ground. In textbook fashion the *Jagdstaffeln* supported the *Schlachtstaffeln* in fighting and attacking ground targets up to 30 May. The fourth day of the attack was the most critical for the Germans because of the appearance of stronger

Some naval landplane pilots served with the *Jagdstaffeln*, including *Oberflugmeister* Schönfelder, who flew with *Jasta* 7 for eighteen months and obtained 13 confirmed victories before he was killed in action on 26 June 1918. He is seen here in front of his Fokker D VII with one of the last British pilots he brought down.

during the same period was 83, approximately 30 of these being caused by enemy action.

During the attack between Montididier and Noyon from 9 to 11 June which was hastily conceived and did not meet with success, *Jagdstaffeln* of both VII and XVIII Armies were used. The units were unfamiliar with the difficult terrain on both sides of Noyon and additionally, most of the *Jagdstaffeln* had come under orders of the *Gruppenkommandos* only one day before the attack began, whereas at least three days' preparation should have been given.

In the second half of June there was still no rest for the fighter pilots despite the pause in the ground fighting. Conditions worsened generally, forcing many of the *Jagdstaffeln* to give up some of their ground personnel to the army and orders were also given to restrict all unnecessary flying due to the low monthly output of fuel, which was given as 7,000 tons in May. In a redistribution of fighter forces, the majority of experienced *Jagdstaffeln* remained in the now enlarged bulge of Amiens–Noyon–Marne in order to fight the ever-stronger enemy formations, and to protect the fighting troops from continuous bombing attacks. A mass employment of fighter units as had been made in previous large-scale attacks was no longer possible.

At this time the members of the *Jagdstaffeln* gave of their finest, well beyond the normal call of duty. They attacked the enemy wherever he could be found, operating sorties lasting two hours each, sometimes four or five times daily. The successes and employment of the *Jagdstaffeln* in the months from April to June mark the highest point of their effect during the whole war. The sheer determination to successfully accomplish their duty did in practical terms reduce the numerical superiority of the enemy to an equitable balance.

On 27 June shortly after 2100 hrs a *kette* of Albatros D Vas from *Jagdstaffel* 46 became engaged in an air fight with twelve Sopwith Camels and S.E.5as at a height of 4,500 metres about 1 kilometre behind the British front line north-west of Albert. At the same instant as *Ltn*. Steinbrecher attacked a Camel he was in turn attacked from behind by another British machine. The strong smell of petrol and the long white trail of vapour that he was leaving behind him told him at once that his fuel

enemy formations, and it became necessary to allocate certain *Jagdstaffeln* to the engagement of enemy squadrons mostly entering the fighting area from the south and west. The focal point of the ground fighting was, from 30 May onwards, on the newly won west front, the main weight of *Jagdstaffeln* employment lying between Villers-Cotterêts and the River Marne. Lively activity of enemy squadrons up to twenty strong and the penetrations of numerous enemy aircraft engaging in the ground fighting, forced on the *Jagdstaffeln* the dual task of fighting both high and low-level enemy aircraft. From 27 May until 18 June 3,323 fighter sorties were undertaken and 130 enemy aeroplanes and 23 balloons brought down. The attrition of D Category aircraft in this army area tank had been hit. He left the scene of the fight in a steep dive and flattened out at about 2,500 metres. Steinbrecher then became aware of intense heat, and suddenly flames engulfed his cockpit. He immediately undid his straps and pushed the stick forward, a move which forced him out of the machine. Momentarily he sat on the fuselage before the airflow forced him back, free of the aircraft. He had always dreaded abandoning his machine because of the danger of hitting the tail unit. In the event he missed it and after a few somersaults his parachute opened. He was hanging head down in the harness, but only a slight movement was needed to regain the normal position. The strong west wind drifted him from west of La Boiselle where he had jumped towards Montauban. Several times he tried to turn round, but every time the torsional effect of the shroud lines spun him back. As he neared the ground he pulled up his legs to bend his knees in order to prevent a hard landing. Despite his precautions the landing was quite heavy and he somersaulted backwards into a shell hole. Steinbrecher had come down 1 kilometre south of Montauban, and about 700 metres from the remains of his burning aeroplane. This was the first successful parachute descent from a German single-seater, and many more were to come in the remaining months of the war (see Explanatory Notes, Appendix II). After a pilot abandoned his disabled machine by parachute his ordeal was far from over; he was still a target and was liable to be shot at both from the ground and from the air. Allied fighters often attacked German pilots hanging in their parachute harnesses, and killed a good number of them. Even after arriving on the ground pilots were sometimes still in danger, especially if they came down in the fighting area, as the experience of *Ltn.* Ernst Udet, *Staffelführer* of *Jagdstaffel* 4, shows. On 29 June at 0715 hrs, Udet took off in a Fokker D VII with his unit on a fighting patrol. Twenty-five minutes later he attacked a French Breguet 14 two-seater flying at a height of 800 metres over Cutry. On his first attack the Breguet turned in towards him and passed underneath, and Udet noticed that the French observer was no longer standing up in his gun-ring and assumed that he had been hit in the first attack. Because of this Udet decided, against his better judgement, on a beam attack. While so doing he suddenly saw the French observer appear in the gun-ring and Udet's machine was hit several times

Ten Fokker D VIIs of *Jagdstaffel* 72 lined up on Bergnicourt aerodrome, July 1918. The machine nearest the camera marked with a large white 'M' on the fuselage sides (and, barely visible, on the centre section of the top wing) is that of the *Staffelführer, Ltn.* Menckhoff.

Vizefeldwebel **Willi Gabriel**, *Jagdstaffel* 11 in his **Fokker D VII (286/18). His final victory score was 11, four of these being obtained on 18 July 1918.**

by the observer's fire. Bullets hit his machine gun and fuel tank and severed the aileron and elevator controls, causing the aircraft to dive out of control. Udet's manipulation of rudder and throttle were insufficient to regain control, and at a height of 500 metres the Fokker entered a vertical dive. Udet decided that it was time to leave the aircraft, undid his straps, stood on the seat and was immediately swept away in the airflow. At the same instant he felt a sudden blow and found that his parachute harness had hooked onto the horn balance of the rudder. Using all his strength he broke off the projection and tumbled free behind the diving machine, somersaulting through the air. Thinking the parachute had failed to open, Udet suddenly became aware of slowing down and shortly afterwards hit the shell-torn earth west of Cutry. His parachute canopy had developed only about 80 metres above the ground. Undoing the parachute harness under machine gun fire, he ran as best he could in an easterly direction. Udet eventually reached positions occupied by the German 16 Infantry Regiment in a coughing and vomiting condition, since he had run more than two kilometres through a French barrage fire of gas and high explosive shells. Several times the blast from the shells had thrown him to the ground and he had been hit on the head and face by flying debris. When the effect of the gas wore off he was able to get back to his aerodrome, and he was airborne again later that same day.

At 2100 hrs on 15 July, *Ltn.* Friedrichs of *Jagdstaffel* 10 took off leading a patrol in Fokker D VII 309/18. As the formation climbed through a height of 1,700 metres, other pilots flying near the leader suddenly noticed that his machine was leaving a trail of white petrol vapour, which was emerging from each side of the fuselage where the fuel tank was located. Friedrichs put his machine into a steep dive and a moment later it burst into flames, just as shots were heard. He immediately abandoned the aircraft but was caught by his parachute harness on the tailplane. The parachute opened and the canopy developed, but the combined weight of pilot and aeroplane overstressed the shroud lines and they parted some 10 centimetres below the main attachments. Friedrichs was killed when the aircraft dived into the ground and burnt itself out. The following day *Ltn.* Bender of *Jagdstaffel* 4 experienced a similar fire in Fokker D VII 2063/18. His parachute jump was successful and he was able to report that at a height of 200 metres, shortly after taking off, he became aware of an unusual heat; he then heard shots and noticed the presence of petrol. Almost immediately his aircraft burst into flames. One hour later *Vizefeldwebel* Meyer of *Jagdstaffel* 45 landed his burning Fokker D VII, which had suddenly burst into flames at a height of 900 metres. The *Staffelführer* of *Jagdstaffel* 68, *Ltn.* Fritz Pütter, died on 10 August from burns received on 16 July when his Fokker D VII burst into flames near Rheims. There were other losses of a similar nature and the initial theory advanced as an explanation for these accidents was leaking fuel tanks, which were known to be of poor manufacture. Leaking fuel was thought to have been ignited by sparks issuing from the short exhaust pipes, or from burnt-through gaskets on the exhaust manifolds. However the true cause of these accidents was the use of extremely unstable phosphorous ammunition and the unusually warm weather at this time. On 22 July an *Idflieg* order was issued forbidding the loading of *Ph-Munition* on Fokker D VII aircraft until further notice (see Explanatory Notes, Appendix II).

The armies involved in the German attack on 15 July on both sides of Rheims were VII Army with fighters from JG 1 and JG 3 plus 10 *Jagdstaffeln* arranged in two *Jagdgruppen*; I Army with 15 *Jagdstaffeln* arranged in three *Jagdgruppen*, and III

Army with fighters from JG 2 and 9 *Jagdstaffeln* arranged in two *Jagdgruppen*. On 15 July these fighter forces possessed aerial superiority from Chateau Thierry to the Argonne. They held the vastly numerically superior enemy in check, continually forced his formations across the Marne to the south and on this day shot down thirty-seven enemy aeroplanes, mostly in VII Army area. German losses amounted to nine aircraft. In front of I and III Armies, the enemy was extremely retiring and avoided all contact that might have led to air fighting.

The employment of enemy squadrons continually increased during the period 16 to 18 July. Their main attacks were directed against the south and west fronts of VII Army, especially against the weakest aspect of the German attack strategy, the rearwards connections over the River Marne. Allied squadrons of from twenty to thirty aeroplanes in close formations destroyed the temporary bridges and landing stages with well-aimed bombs, and thus cut the lifeline of the attacking troops who were south of the river. Heavy losses were incurred in infantry columns close to the North Marne bank from anti-personnel bombs, which exploded at various heights above the ground. The massive enemy formations threw themselves against the *Jagdstaffeln* with exemplary sacrifice, yet it was possible for the German fighter units, especially *Jagdgeschwadern* 1 and 3, to stem the tide. During continuous attacks against the Marne bridge at Dormans they brought down twenty-five enemy aircraft. More serious and dangerous was the situation on 17 July: bombing attacks were repeated almost unabated against the Marne bridges. *Jagdstaffeln* were airborne seven times during the day and fought bitter air battles absolutely contesting the supremacy of the enemy. They were able to force the mass of enemy squadrons back over the Marne, and produced victory scores never before equalled. The enemy lost 113 aeroplanes and 6 balloons against the loss of 27 German aeroplanes during the period from 16 to 23 July.

On 18 July, following a terrific bombardment, the French launched a counter-attack supported by tanks, from the thick woods near Villers Cotterêts on both sides of the Aisne river against IX Army and

continued on page 33

Oberleutnant pilot, formerly of the 1st Leibhusaren. He wears a soft peaked cap with band and piping in his old regimental colours, and the hussar 'Attila' tunic with rich, black-flecked frogging. His shoulder-straps have underlay in regimental colour, a gold rank pip and the gold wing-and-propeller badge of his new service. The Prussian pilot's badge and the Iron Cross are worn. Long gaiters are typical casual service wear.

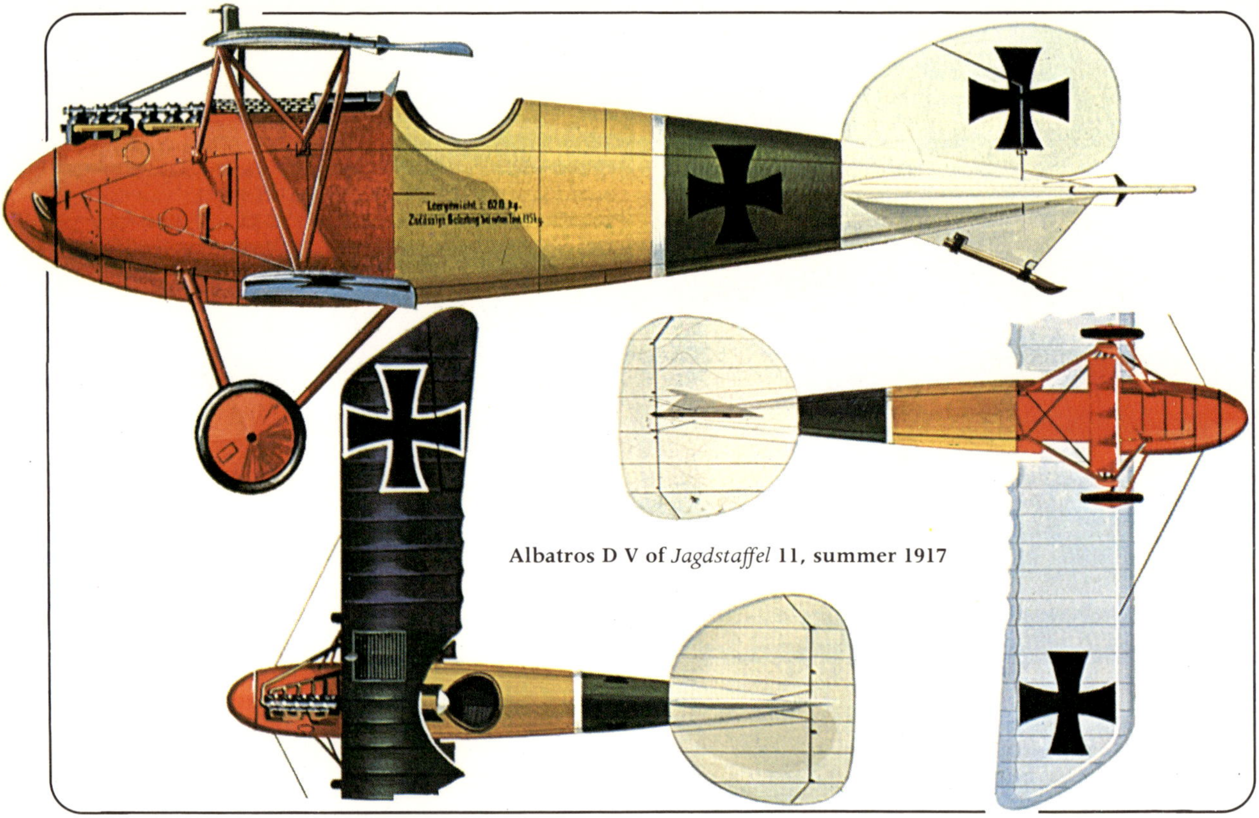

Albatros D V of *Jagdstaffel* 11, summer 1917

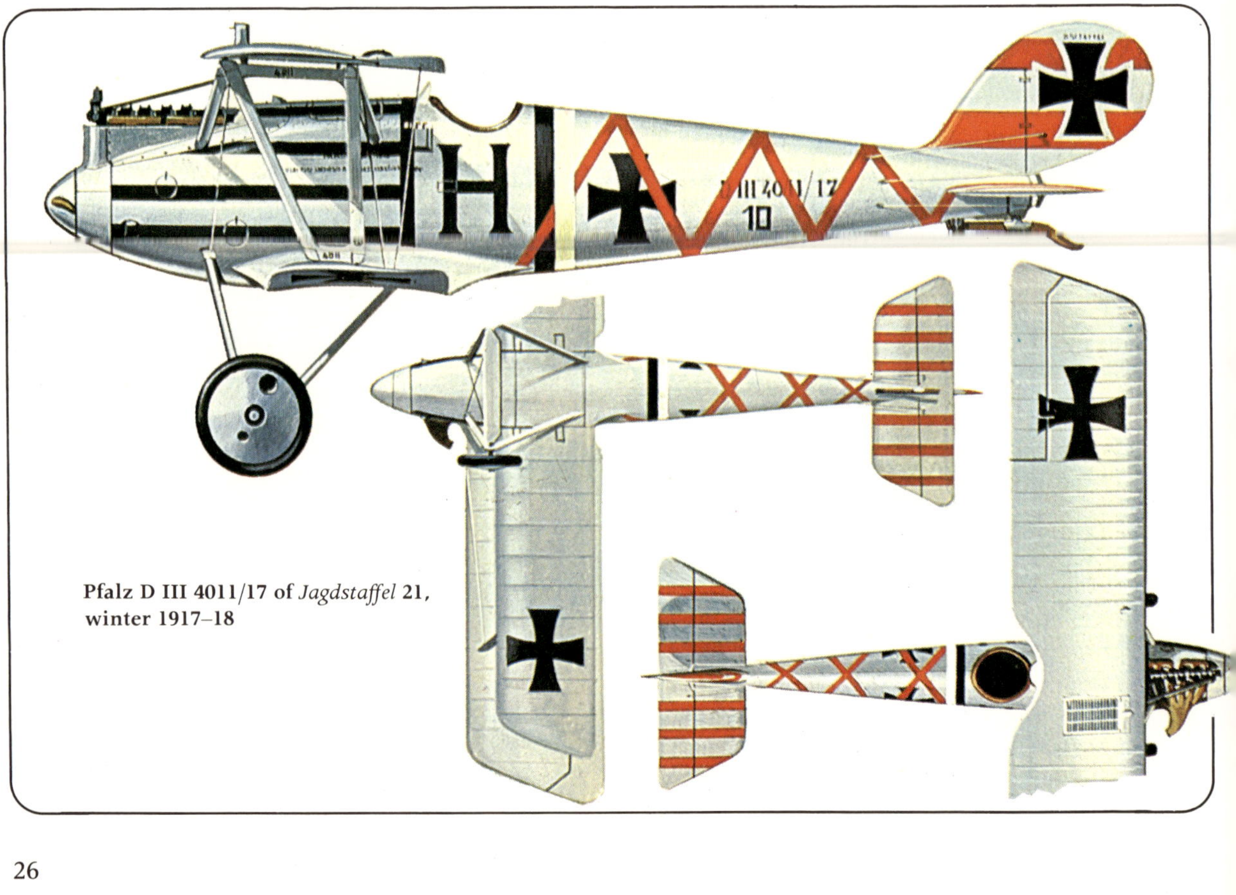

Pfalz D III 4011/17 of *Jagdstaffel* 21,
winter 1917–18

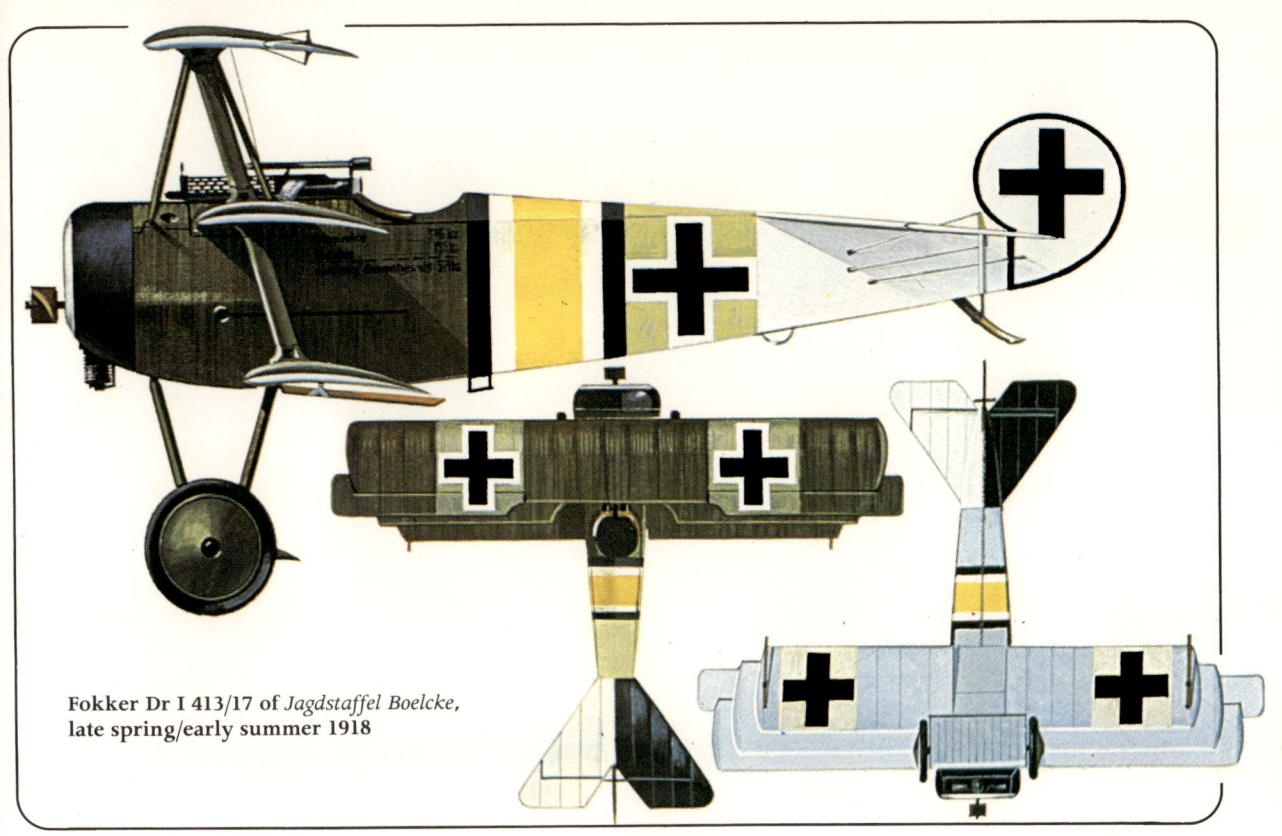

Fokker Dr I 413/17 of *Jagdstaffel Boelcke*,
late spring/early summer 1918

OPPOSITE TOP: **Albatros D V** flown by *Ltn*. **Franz Müller** of *Jagdstaffel* 11, summer 1917. The widespread use of lilac as an upper surface camouflage shade followed the *Idflieg* order dated 12 April 1917, which specifically stated that only this colour was to be used with dark green for such purposes, the use of reddish-brown used by most manufacturers until that time being discontinued. The red area shown on the forward fuselage became standard on machines of *Jasta* 11, extending to struts and wheel covers to comprise the unit markings. Manfred von Richthofen himself decreed that the top and bottom surfaces of the tail unit were the best positions to display personal identification colours although pilots were still allowed to flaunt an additional personal marking if they so wished. Müller's machine shows the use of green and white fuselage bands for this purpose.

OPPOSITE BOTTOM: **Pfalz D III** 4011/17 flown by *Ltn*. **Fritz Höhn** of *Jagdstaffel* 21, winter 1917–18. The unit marking was the black and white band behind the cockpit, the other decoration being the pilot's personal choice. At the time, Höhne was specializing in attacks on observation balloons and it was thought that the unusual combination of personal markings were intended to break up the outline of his machine to enemy gunners by optical illusion. Also unusual on the machines of *Jasta* 21 was the

allocation of small individual numbers, carried in this case below the fuselage serial number. The overall silver finish of the Pfalz D III was in direct contrast to the terrain camouflage schemes carried by most other fighter types and was said to possess 'sky camouflage' properties.

ABOVE: **Fokker Dr I** 413/17 flown by *Ltn*. **Carl Bolle**, *Staffelführer* of *Jagdstaffel Boelcke*, late spring/early summer 1918. The black and white rear fuselage, tailplane and elevators and black engine cowling with white front panel comprised the unit markings, with Bolle's own markings in the form of multi-coloured fuselage bands. In this case the broad yellow represented the pilot's old regiment, Kürassier Regiment von Seydlitz No. 7. Standard finish for Fokker Dr Is was all top and side surfaces streaked in a green/brown shade, the streaky effect being vertical on the fuselage sides, almost chordwise on the wings and oblique on the fuselage decking and tail unit. Undersides were light blue and the Iron Cross form of the national insignia with a white painted background was applied at usual locations and directly to the clear doped natural fabric on wing undersides. In March/April 1918 these crosses had their backgrounds overpainted in the field in the manner shown, the subject machine using a light green for this purpose. Factory finished inter-plane struts were usually blue but in this case they have been overpainted.

27

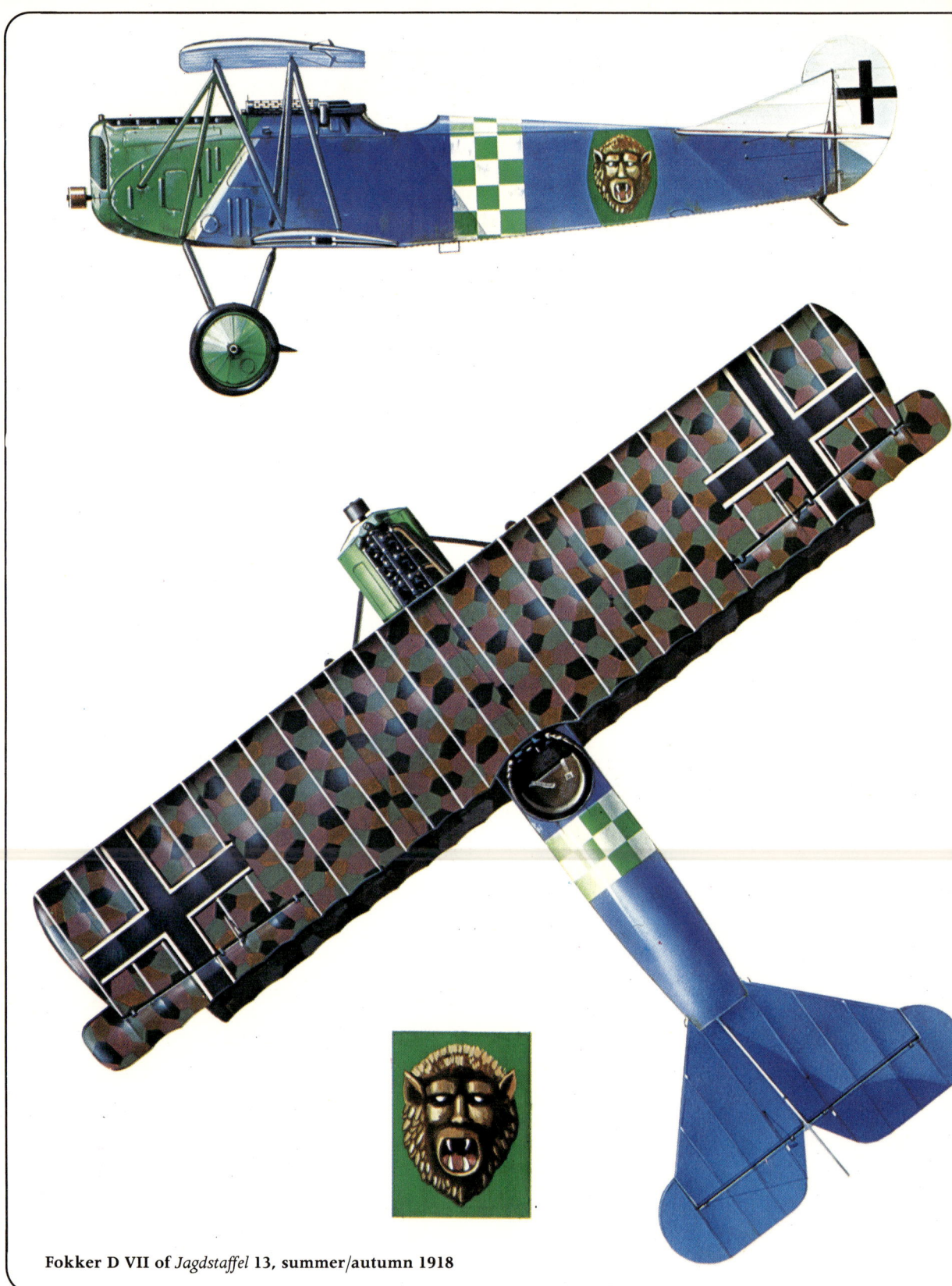

Fokker D VII of *Jagdstaffel* **13, summer/autumn 1918**

PAGES 28–29: OAW-built Fokker D VII flown by *Ltn.* Franz Büchner, *Staffelführer, Jasta* 13, summer/autumn 1918. A native of Saxony, Büchner used the green and white Saxon colours as shown. A green nose was the unit marking which initially ended in a vertical line just ahead of the cockpit; when Büchner took over the unit, the green was reduced as shown and appropriately, he added a white stripe to the unit colour. Overpainting of fuselage, tailplane and elevators in blue was introduced by *Hptm.* Berthold, *Kommandeur* of JG 2 of which *Jasta* 13 was part. Wing treatment was common on OAW-built D VIIs.

BELOW: Albatros D Va flown by *Ltn.* Ernst Udet, *Staffelführer, Jasta* 37, winter 1917/18, showing the unit markings of black/white striped tailplane and elevators. When he became *Staffelführer*, Udet introduced the black fuselage, fin/rudder, strut and wheel cover trim. Unit pilots used fuselage symbols, mainly white, and large numerals (1–14) on either side of the nose and below the wings as personal identification. Udet carried the abbreviation of his fiancée's name and instead of a nose number, a chevron. The white 'U' under the wings simplified the corroboration of victories for ground observers and two chordwise white upper wing bands commonly denoted a leader, as did tail streamers. Upper wings in five colour printed pattern fabric (1), lower wings in lighter material (2).

OPPOSITE TOP: (A) personal marking, OAW-built Albatros D III flown by *Vzfw.* Boldt, *Jasta* 31. Aircraft had short white bars around fuselage aft of cross: camouflage was lilac/olive green uppersurfaces of wings and tail unit; undersides light sky blue. Fuselage natural plywood finish. (B) Kiel coat of arms as personal marking, *Ltn.* Leptien, Albatros D Va, *Jasta* 63. Nose to tail black diamonds on natural plywood fuselage was unit marking; wings in pattern fabric. (C) Family coat of arms as personal marking, Fokker Dr I, *Ltn.* Hasso von Wedel, *Jasta* 14. Flanking black/white stripe was nose to tail unit marking. Iron crosses in usual locations on white fields, but fuselage crosses painted out with dark green dope. Standard airframe finish. (D) Personal marking, *Uffz.* Piel, Fokker D VII, *Jasta* 13. Green nose and blue overpainted fuselage/tail unit with vertical colour division ahead of cockpit. Wing surfaces, 4-colour pattern fabric (E) *Jasta* 18 Fokker D VII, *Ltn.* Günther von Büren. All upper/side surfaces of fuselage, and upper wing surfaces, red; rear fuselage/tail unit white with black raven (der Rabe) denoting *Staffelführer, Ltn.* August Raben. (F) Mythical Valkyrie helmet as personal marking. *Oblt.* Hermann Dahlmann, *Adjutant*, JG 3 on a BMW-powered Fokker D VII. Black nose; fuselage/tailplane/elevators striped black/white as unit marking, *Jasta* 26, part of JG 3. All wing surfaces in 4-colour printed fabric.

OPPOSITE BOTTOM: Transportation trailer, used by *Jasta* 19, autumn 1917.

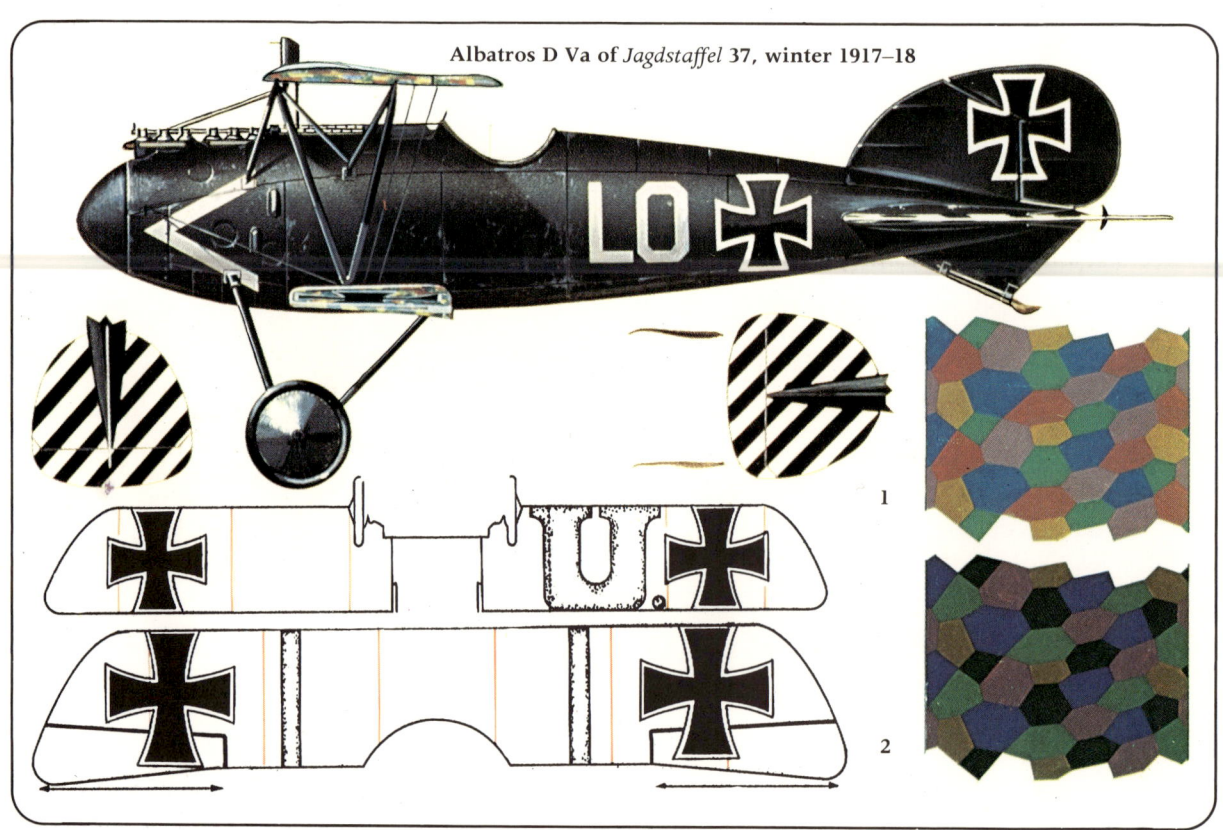

Albatros D Va of *Jagdstaffel* 37, winter 1917–18

A

B

C

D

E

F

Transportation trailer of *Jagdstaffel* 19, autumn 1917

Leutnant pilot, ex-12th Ulans, in captured British flying coat—a popular item—with added fur collar. Cap band and piping in cornflower blue and white date from his old regiment. Puttees and ankle boots often replaced top-boots for everyday wear.

Pilot in full flying clothing with Heinecke parachute harness, 1918. The special issue Fliegerhosen are worn with a private-purchase leather coat, helmet and goggles. The harness is reinforced with leather and has extra-broad leg straps; some early harnesses failed. The pilot sat on the 'chute' and the static line was attached permanently to the aircraft.

the right wing of VII Army. The enemy quickly gained ground and it was not until 20 July that German reserves managed to stop the advance in the hills to the south-west of Soissons.

The immediate result of the French attack was the final cancellation of the German plan to attack Rheims and mount an offensive against the British in Flanders, and it forced a change along the whole front to that of defence. The employment of Allied bombing squadrons in almost continuous waves at medium altitude had a serious effect on the German retreat. These formations were escorted by many fighter aeroplanes which either circled over the attacking bombers or mounted strong patrols between Soissons and the Marne. This was a most difficult day for the *Jagdstaffeln* in their fight against such massive numerical superiority. The rapid appraisal of the situation and the decision to concentrate the German fighters in support of the fighting troops was a commendable action by the leaders of the fighter forces, who saw this as their most important task. *Jagdgeschwader* 3, completely engaged in the ground fighting for the first time, attacked enemy batteries south of the Aisne in a general free-for-all and put them out of action for long periods. Owing to the countless enemy formations at higher altitudes it was not possible to seriously interfere with them or turn them back with the small number of *Jagdstaffeln* available for this duty. However, the fighter pilots, aggressive, courageous and with their continual participation, turned this unhappy day for the German Army into a shining success for the *Jagdstaffeln*. During the day thirty-four enemy aeroplanes were destroyed, fourteen of them falling to pilots of JG 1.

One of the pilots who contributed to this impressive total was *Vizefeldwebel* Willi Gabriel of *Jagdstaffel* 11. In a day of hectic air fighting he brought down four enemy machines on 18 July. Following the morning fighting patrol under the new *Kommandeur* of JG 1, Oblt. Göring, Gabriel did not land but returned to the lines. He stalked a formation of Spads and shot down the rearmost machine from only 50 metres range, but he was then engaged by the remaining eight aircraft. During the fight he managed to shoot down another and eventually the Spads withdrew. Returning to the aerodrome at Beugneux, Gabriel saw a formation of

Aerodrome look-out post, *Jagdstaffel* 58. Equipment includes a telephone under the roofed structure at left, a Goerz rangefinder on tripod stand and air-driven Klaxon type horn operated by a large oxygen bottle.

Breguet two-seaters far above him. He climbed rapidly to their level in his BMW-powered Fokker D VII, and successfully engaged the rearmost machine. It fell out of control to hit the the ground about a kilometre from the aerodrome. Although Gabriel had scored three victories, Göring reprimanded him for going off on his own; but following an afternoon patrol Gabriel again left the formation and was able to destroy a two-seater Spad attacking German infantry. Although such tactics could be rewarding, they were highly dangerous at this stage of the war, and Gabriel's disregard for discipline resulted in his posting away from JG 1.

*   *   *

Three factors altered the critical situation from 19 July onwards: supporting *Jagdstaffeln* from I and III Armies were brought into action and the enemy became much more reticent in his aerial operations, due possibly to the losses he had suffered since 15 July; and *Jagdgeschwader* 2 from III Army strengthened the fighter disposition on the west and south sectors of the front. These moves resulted in a rapid balance being achieved which greatly helped the retreating German forces. Once again it was possible for large numbers of fighter aeroplanes to be directly employed in the ground fighting and concentrations of troops, cavalry, and motor transport were attacked by single-seaters working with the *Schlachtstaffeln*. On 22 July, forty-one enemy aeroplanes were brought down for the loss of two German machines. The strengthened German fighter force was now superior to that of the enemy and the well-flown close formations of the Allied squadrons were usually broken up and mostly forced back over the front line. In the area of VII Army enemy losses in aeroplanes and balloons totalled 200 between 15 and 31 July.

Following the fighting on the Marne the OHL did not expect further immediate large-scale enemy attacks. The Allies on the other hand, while appreciating that the time was not yet ripe for a final decisive battle, knew that they must not allow the Germans time to recoup following the Marne success. The Allied target chosen was the bulge in the front between the Ancre and the Oise rivers. When it came on 8 August the attack took the Germans by surprise, the main reasons being that the whole front was so strongly reinforced with implements of attack that it was difficult to know when a particular front was being weakened or strengthened, and the attack was not carried out by means of strength distributed in depth but from the front itself. The use of light tanks also made it easy for the enemy to conceal his intentions. Aerial reconnaissance in July was not carried out with the same regularity as hitherto and early in August ceased almost completely.

Early on the morning of 8 August, after a short preliminary bombardment, the Allies attacked and quickly overran the forward positions of II Army and the German troops were put to flight. The enemy possessed complete aerial superiority, and *Hptm.* Haehnelt, the *Kofl* of II Army, quickly organized fighter assistance from other armies. Soon *Jagdstaffeln* were engaged in fierce air fighting, especially against enemy bombing squadrons mounting determined attacks against bridges over the River Somme intending to cut off the large number of German troops west of the river. The intervention by the German fighters prevented the destruction of these bridges, and the enemy lost sixty-two aeroplanes on the first day of the fighting. A further eighty-two enemy machines had been brought down by 11 August; thus in four days of air fighting in this area the Allies lost 144 aeroplanes compared to German losses of 30 machines.

The influx of fighter forces from other army areas meant that the aerial situation improved and the absolute superiority of the enemy was usually only apparent during formation attacks of massive proportions. From 15 August *Jagdgeschwadern* and *Jagdgruppen* effectively broke up these formations and forced them to jettison their bombs before they reached their targets. Severe losses in material and personnel and the new low fuel ration in the fighter units, where only 150 litres per day were allowed per serviceable aeroplane, restricted the effectiveness of the *Jagdstaffeln*. There was, however, no weakening of morale and the standard of skill displayed by the pilots was just as high in the last months of the war as it had been at any time during the four year struggle. Targets of opportunity on the ground were normally sought out and attacked by aircraft up on offensive patrols when no enemy aircraft could be found. On 23 August *Oblt.* Greim, *Gruja* 10 and *Staffelführer Jagdstaffel* 34b, led his pilots on such a patrol over the fighting area. *Vizefeldwebel* Pütz, working with his commanding officer, circled over the battle area at a height of 500 metres and saw two tanks advancing amid the smoke and shell bursts. The two pilots decided immediately to attack the metal monsters, especially since their machine-gun belts held *Panzer-Munition* (armour piercing) as well as the ordinary ball, tracer and phosphorous rounds. Greim made his first attack, aiming at the side of the tank, Pütz following suit and attacking the other tank in the same manner. Initially Greim only used the machine gun that was belted with armour piercing rounds, then at close range brought the other gun into use as well. However, the tanks continued on their way undisturbed by the aerial assault. The Germans had in fact received the worst of the encounter, since machine gun fire from the tanks had been unusually accurate. Greim then decided to attack from above, and in a few moments both he and Pütz had climbed to 500 metres. They throttled back and made vertical dives on the tanks, firing both guns. These attacks continued to very close range and the aircraft pulled out only just over the tanks. Greim realized that he had not been shot at during his dive, and it was only afterwards that he saw that the tank had stopped. The tank that had been attacked by Pütz had also come to a halt. Suspiciously, the pilots watched the stationary monsters for some time, but there was no sign of life and they flew back to their aerodrome at Foucaucourt. Shortly after they

Five Fokker D VIIs of *Jasta* 11 about to leave Beugneux aerodrome, July 1918. *Vizefeldwebel* Gabriel at extreme left is donning flying kit and the pilot being assisted with his flying clothing by the second machine is *Oblt.* von Wedel, who later became the *Staffelführer* of *Jasta* 11 and was credited with 11 victories.

landed, a report came in from the front line via *Grufl* 14 that confirmed their successes. Both tanks were *hors de combat*. One became the seventh victory for *Vizefeldwebel* Pütz, while the other was number twenty-three on *Oblt.* Greim's victory list.

Despite the restrictions mentioned and the desperation of the retreat the *Jagdstaffeln* never ceased to perform their duties to the upmost of their abilities. That these duties were highly effective is reflected in the victory scores that some units produced at this time. In a day of particularly fierce air fighting on 2 September, *Jagdgeschwader* 3 brought down twenty-six enemy aeroplanes without loss, and in the seven day period from 12 September, *Jagdgeschwader* 2 engaged in eighty-one successful combats for the loss of only two of its own machines.

In addition to their daylight activities, single-seater machines were operated at night against enemy bombers, and as far as is known *Jagdstaffeln* 24 and 73 were the most successful at this nocturnal occupation. *Leutnant* Fritz Anders, the *Staffelführer* of *Jasta* 73, recorded five confirmed victories at night and was probably the most successful German night fighter pilot.

The advantages of the permanent grouping of *Jagdstaffeln* had been demonstrated many times during the previous year, and on 10 October their number was increased yet again when the Bavarian *Jagdstaffeln* 23, 32, 34, and 35 became *Jagdgeschwader* 4 under the overall command of *Oblt.* Ritter von Schleich.

Marine Feld-Jagdstaffeln

The *Marine-Feld-Jagdstaffel* operating from Aer-trycke aerodrome in Flanders during the summer of 1917 had scored some thirty victories by the time it moved to Coolkerke aerodrome on 10 September. A second unit under *Oblt.* Reusch appears to have been merely a holding unit and it was not until 18 July that it was given the official designation of II *Marine-Feld-Jagdstaffel*. Equipped with Pfalz D III machines, it moved to Coolkerke on 19 October and joined forces with the Albatros single-seaters of Sachsenberg's unit, now officially named I *Marine-Feld-Jagdstaffel*. These two units operated as the *Marine Jagdgruppe* with *Ltn.* Osterkamp as *Staffelführer* of the second unit from 21 March 1918, and moved to Jabbecke aerodrome on 3 April. On 23 June III *Marine-Feld-Jagdstaffel* was formed out of the first two units under the command of *Ltn.* Brockhoff. During this time Fokker D VIIs were received by the first unit, some machines of the same type going to Osterkamp's unit, while the now surplus Albatros D Va were allocated to Brockhoff's *Staffel*. The *Marine Jagdgruppe* had scored ninety-seven confirmed victories by 30 June, the leading pilots being Sachsenberg and Osterkamp, both of whom were later awarded the *Pour le mérite*. Previously, another marine land fighter unit (*Seefrontstaffel*) had been formed in August 1917 for the defence of the Flanders sea front under the command of *Ltn. zur See* Rolshoven. This formation was eventually divided up into the I and II *Seefrosta*

Leutnant **Loewenhardt**, *Staffelführer* of *Jagdstaffel* 10 (left) and *Leutnant* Friedrichs with a captured Spad 13. Both these pilots were fine air fighters, Friedrichs specializing in attacking observation balloons, 16 of which were included in his final victory score of 21 when he fell on 15 July 1918. Loewenhardt collided with *Leutnant* Wentz from *Jasta* 11 during an air fight on 10 August 1918. Both pilots jumped by parachute, Wentz landing safely despite two failures to the Heinecke harness webbing straps, but Loewenhardt, with 54 confirmed victories, was killed.

and late in 1918 these units were renamed IV and V *Marine-Feld-Jagdstaffel* respectively and joined the *Marine Jagdgruppe*, which then used the designation *Marine-Feld-Jagdgeschwader*.

Fokker D VII in flight. Said to be the machine of *Leutnant* Loewenhardt, *Staffelführer* of *Jagdstaffel* 10, it is flying leader's streamers from both wing tips and rudder.

OTHER FRONTS

Balkans

Single-seaters from *Kampfgeschwader* 1 and *Flieger Abteilung* 30 were combined into one unit in June 1917: *Jagdstaffel* Vardar. *Staffelführer* was *Oblt.* Böhm and on 30 June the official designation of *Jagdstaffel* 38 was issued. This unit and *Jagdstaffel* 25 were the only German single-seater units to serve in Macedonia.

Eastern Front

On the Eastern Front two fighter aircraft were usually allocated to the two-seater units on active sectors, these being in excess of their normal establishment. These loosely dispersed fighter elements were combined into *Kampfeinsitzerstaffeln* as required and eventually three main formations emerged, designated *Jagdfliegerstaffeln* 1–3. On 5 May 1917, *Jagdfliegerstaffel* 2 was disbanded and combined with *Flieger Abteilung* (A) 230, and *Jagdfliegerstaffeln* 1 and 3 were absorbed into *Flieger Abteilungen* (A) 220 and 242 respectively. All Eastern Front fighters were encompassed in *Jasta Ober Ost* on 15 June and on the southern sector of the front a formation named *Jagdfliegerstaffel Süd* was created. Eventually, late in 1917, the designation of *Jagdstaffel* 81 was given to the amalgamation of all these fighters under the command of *Rittmeister* Wulff. With the cessation of hostilities against Russia, *Jasta* 81 moved to the Western Front early in 1918 and later served as a component unit of *Jagdgruppe* 5 in May 1918.

Italy

On the Italian Front *Jagdstaffeln* 1, 31, and 39 flew alongside Austro-Hungarian units against British and Italian forces. Early in March 1918 these *Jasta* returned to the Western Front for the German offensive and remained in that theatre of operations until the end of the war.

Palestine

Six German two-seater units (*Feldflieger Abteilungen* 300–303, 304 (b) and 305, part of the Yilderim Army) had two Albatros D III single-seaters each on their establishments and had just started operations when the third Battle of Gaza opened, forcing them to withdraw further into Palestine. In January 1918 all the single-seaters were collected into one unit under *Oblt.* Felmy and named *Jagdstaffel* 300. The need for a fighter unit in Palestine had been apparent for some time, and in Germany the *Jagdstaffel* due to receive the number 55 was redesignated *Jagdstaffel* 1 (F) and was dispatched to Palestine under the command of *Ltn.* Meierdirks. Equipped with Albatros D Va machines fitted with twin radiators to cater for the higher than normal temperatures, the unit reached Djenin at the end of March 1918. Despite tropicalization, the Albatros D Va proved to be unsuitable in this theatre of operations and Albatros D IIIs were normally used, although later, some suitably modified Albatros D Va did see service again. Later *Jasta* 300 combined its resources with the new formation and appears to have operated under the dual designation of *Jasta* 1 (F) and *Jasta* 300. Losses were heavy, replacement of men and material extremely difficult, and the story of this formation is a continual record of retreat and defeat. Although many acts of bravery were performed by its members, against the vastly superior enemy forces there could only be one ending. In July only seven aircraft were serviceable, and despite the arrival of replacements this

Fokker D VII of *Jagdgeschwader* 2 on Chéry-les-Pouilly aerodrome, August 1918. The machines in the foreground are from *Jagdstaffel* 15, that with the winged arrow marking being the aircraft of the *Staffelführer, Ltn.* Veltjens.

Jagdstaffel Boelcke. **Left to right**: *Gefreiter* **Mynerek**, *Leutnant* **Löffler**, *Leutnant* **Heinz**, *Leutnant* **Hoffmann**, *Leutnant Freiherr* **Wolframm von Gudenberg** (*Adjutant*), *Leutnant* **Bolle** (*Staffelführer*), *Oberleutnant* **von Griesheim**, *Leutnant* **Klausenberg**, *Leutnant* **Bassenge**, *Vizefeldwebel* **Jentsch** and *Leutnant* **Lindenberger**. When the photograph was taken on 28 August 1918 to celebrate the award of the *Pour le mérite* to the *Staffelführer*, this famous unit's score stood at **260** confirmed victories—a total that increased to **336** by the Armistice.

figure had dropped to five in September. Following the fall of Aleppo in October, all personnel were interned as prisoners of war and did not return to Germany until 31 March 1919. On the demobilization list the unit is shown as *Jagdstaffel* 300.

Pilots of *Jagdstaffel* 12, August 1918, shown in the formation position they normally occupied in the air. **Left to right:** *Leutnant* **Greven**, *Flieger* **Wilke**, *Gefreiter* **Rossbach**, *Leutnant* **Stölting**, *Leutnant* **Koch**, *Leutnant* **Becker** (*Staffelführer*), *Leutnant* **Neckel**, *Leutnant* **Besser**, *Leutnant* **Muhs**, *Sergeant* **Wittchen** and *Leutnant* **Bock**. At centre back is *Leutnant* **von Wurmb**, the unit *Adjutant*.

Rumania

In mid-May 1917 some Halberstadt D II machines were received by *Armee Flug Park* 9 in Bucharest and flown during the summer, mostly by two-seater pilots from *Feldflieger Abteilungen* 42 and 38. No permanent fighter unit resulted from this activity however.

*   *   *

The order to lay down their arms was, for the pilots of the *Jagdstaffeln*, unbelievable. Compelled to stop fighting, the German fighter force was certainly not a demoralized defeated foe—it was the Armistice that forced them out of the air not the Allied airmen—and worse was still to come. The order to deliver certain single-seaters to the enemy, especially all Fokker D VIIs, was too much for some members of the *Jagdstaffeln*. Some units maintained that they never received the order, and flew their machines back to Germany or as far in that direction as the shortage of fuel would allow. Other machines were damaged or destroyed on their last operational aerodromes.

Discipline in the *Jagdstaffeln* was, however, still of a far higher order than that of the weary battalions that trudged homewards to Germany. Many aircraft were flown to the designated aerodromes to be handed over, and it was with heavy hearts that pilots and mechanics took leave of their beloved aeroplanes that suddenly meant so much to them. Taxying accidents and heavy landings made at the collection centres ensured that some of the fighters would not fly again. Other units arrived in impeccable formation in a last defiant gesture, and as they taxied up to the Allied Commission waiting for them, the machines came to rest in an orderly line. As the engines kicked over their last compressions, the onlookers could see that each machine had been marked with the number of enemy aeroplanes it had destroyed.

Right:
Nine Fokker E V parasol monoplane fighters and four Fokker D VIIs of *Jasta* **6 lined up on Bernes aerodrome, August 1918. The first parasol victory was scored by** *Leutnant* **Rolff of this unit on 16 August but he was killed three days later as a result of one of the structural failures that caused the E V to be withdrawn from the front. Strengthened and redesignated D VIII, the type saw action again in the last few weeks of hostilities.**

APPENDIX I The Aircraft

Albatros D V/D Va (160hp Mercedes D III or 180hp Mercedes D IIIa)

Wingspan	9·05m	(29ft $8\frac{1}{4}$in)	
Length	7·33m	(24ft $0\frac{5}{8}$in)	
Height	2·7m	(8ft $10\frac{1}{4}$in)	
Maximum speed	165km/h	(103mph)	
Weight empty	687kg	(1,511lb)	
Weight loaded	937kg	(2,061lb)	
Rate of climb	1,000m	(3,280ft)	4min
	2,000m	(6,560ft)	8·8min
	3,000m	(9,840ft)	14·8min
	4,000m	(13,120ft)	22·8min
	5,000m	(16,400ft)	35·0min

Pfalz D III/D IIIa (160hp Mercedes D III or 180hp Mercedes D IIIa)

Wingspan	9·4m	(30ft $10\frac{1}{8}$in)	
Length	6·95m	(22ft $9\frac{3}{4}$in)	
Height	2·67m	(8ft $9\frac{1}{8}$in)	
Maximum speed	165km/h	(103mph)	
Weight empty	695kg	(1,529lb)	
Weight loaded	915kg	(2,013lb)	
Rate of climb	1,000m	(3,280ft)	3·25min
	2,000m	(6,560ft)	7·25min
	3,000m	(9,840ft)	11·75min
	4,000m	(13,120ft)	20·18min
	5,000m	(16,400ft)	33·0min

Fokker Dr I (110hp Oberursel UR 11)

Wingspan	7·19m	(23ft $7\frac{3}{8}$in)	
Length	5·77m	(18ft $11\frac{1}{8}$in)	
Height	2·95m	(8ft $8\frac{1}{8}$in)	
Maximum speed	156km/h	(97mph)	
Weight empty	406kg	(893lb)	
Weight loaded	586kg	(1,289lb)	
Rate of climb	1,000m	(3,280ft)	3min
	2,000m	(6,560ft)	6min
	3,000m	(9,840ft)	10min
	4,000m	(13,120ft)	15min
	5,000m	(16,400ft)	24min

Fokker D VII (160hp Mercedes D III or 185hp BMW 111a)

Wingspan	8·9m	(29ft $3\frac{1}{2}$in)	
Length	7·0m	(22ft $11\frac{5}{8}$in)	
Height	2·75m	(9ft $2\frac{1}{4}$in)	
Maximum speed	185km/h	(115mph)	
Weight empty	700kg	(1,540lb)	
Weight loaded	850kg	(1,620lb)	
Rate of climb	1,000m	(3,280ft)	2min
(BMW 111a)	2,000m	(6,560ft)	4min
	3,000m	(9,840ft)	8min
	4,000m	(13,120ft)	11min
	5,000m	(16,400ft)	15min
	6,000m	(19,680ft)	20min

Siemens D IV (160hp Siemens und Halske 111a)

Wingspan	8·35m	(27ft $4\frac{3}{4}$in)	
Length	5·7m	(18ft $8\frac{1}{2}$in)	
Height	2·72m	(8ft 11in)	
Maximum speed	190km/h	(119mph)	
Weight empty	540kg	(1,190lb)	
Weight loaded	735kg	(1,620 lb)	
Rate of climb	1,000m	(3,280ft)	1·8min
	2,000m	(6,560ft)	3·7min
	3,000m	(9,840ft)	6·4min
	4,000m	(13,120ft)	9·1min
	5,000m	(16,400ft)	12·1min
	6,000m	(19,680ft)	15·5min

Fokker EV/D VIII (110hp Oberursel UR 11)

Wingspan	8·34m	(27ft $4\frac{3}{4}$in)	
Length	5·86m	(19ft $2\frac{3}{4}$in)	
Height	2·6m	(8ft $6\frac{3}{8}$in)	
Maximum speed	204km/h	(127mph)	
Weight empty	405kg	(893lb)	
Weight loaded	605kg	(1,334lb)	
Rate of climb	1,000m	(3,280ft)	2min
	2,000m	(6,560ft)	4·5min
	3,000m	(9,840ft)	7·5min
	4,000m	(13,120ft)	10·75min
	5,000m	(16,400ft)	16·0min

Pilots of *Jasta* 4 on Escaufort aerodrome, 5 September 1918.
Left to right: *Leutnant* **Kraut**, *Leutnant* **Hildebrandt**, *Flieger*
Rohde, *Leutnant* **von Winterfeld**, *Leutnant* **Koepsch** (*Acting*
Staffelführer), *Leutnant* **Maushake** (on wing), *Leutnant* **von**
Gluszewski and *Leutnant* **Bender**. Note the different types
of Heinecke parachute harness worn.

APPENDIX II
Explanatory Notes
1. Development of Fighter Aircraft

A state of stagnation had existed in the development of
the German fighter aeroplane ever since the appearance
of the excellent Albatros D III, which had reigned
supreme over the Western Front during the spring of
1917. It was hoped that the LFG Roland D II using the
higher powered Argus 180hp engine would be an
improvement on the Albatros D III, but poor performance at altitude, initially thought to have been caused
by an engine fault, was found to be due to bad
aerodynamic design. In an attempt to further improve the
performance of the Albatros D III, a lightened version
was produced designated Albatros D V. Although this
machine had an empty weight of approximately 50
kilograms less than the D III, its performance was no
better, and the lightening process had robbed the basic
design of the ruggedness that had been one of the
attributes of the Albatros D III. The D V was not a
popular aircraft with pilots, and its use in numbers

during the latter half of 1917 (513 machines at the front at
the end of December) was a contributory factor in the loss
of fighting ability of the *Jagdstaffeln*. A modified version
was soon to appear as the Albatros D Va and this machine
would be used until the end of the war by some units.
Pfalz Flugzeug-Werke GmbH produced its D III model
powered by the 160hp Mercedes engine, but the
performance was not greatly different from the Albatros
D III/D V, in fact some handling properties were not as
good. Structural problems were not absent on these
designs, the most prevalent being found on the Vee-
strutter Albatros. This varied from rib failures accom-
panied by shedding fabric to the complete detachment of
major components in flight. While these airframe
shortcomings were generally overcome by beefing-up
structures and improved inspection standards during
manufacture, it was realized that better performance
could only come from higher powered engines, and a
clause in the *Amerikaprogramm* of mid-1917 had given
emphasis to this requirement. While experiments went
ahead with stationary engines, the continued use of the
rotary engine was evaluated. Such powerplants had
given good service in light airframes, but as early as the
autumn of 1916 it had been foreseen that the shortage of
castor oil would impose problems for machines powered
by these engines, which consumed large amounts of
castor oil. Tests were conducted running rotary engines
on mineral oil and the Le Rhône type of engine was run

on this oil without undue trouble except for the excessive build-up of carbon. However, it was considered that rotary engines with crankcase induction would not be suitable for conversion. As a result Óberursel began to phase out its engines built on the Gnôme principle and concentrate, with Siemens, on the development of 120, 140 and 160hp rotary engines modelled on the Le Rhône. Following the appearance of the Sopwith Triplane at the front, German constructors began to devote themselves to designs of a similar configuration. The first usable design was the Fokker Dr I, which first appeared in July 1917. Production was delayed due to the lack of rotary engines, and some of the first machines to reach the front were powered by captured Le Rhône engines. Eventually Oberursel made Le Rhône copies in the form of the Oberursel UR II. Structural problems also affected the delivery of this machine and it was not until the winter of 1917/18 that Fokker Dr Is reached the front in number. The lubrication oil used on the Fokker Dr I was by this time a highly suspect substance known as *castor-ersatz*, an oil that certainly contributed to the unreliability record of the Oberursel UR II. The *Amerikaprogramm* clause which focused attention on the development of fighter aeroplanes was responsible for a spate of designs which were flown in comparative test flights at Adlershof aerodrome near Berlin. Front line pilots flew these machines to test their manoeuvrability, and in the final analysis much emphasis was placed on their reports. The outright winner in the first fighter competition held in January/February 1918 was Fokker's cantilever biplane V 11, a machine produced as the Fokker D VII. It became the best German fighter of the war and formed the main equipment of the *Jagdstaffeln* at the Armistice. Other designs that emerged from later fighter competitions were the Siemens D IV; the Pfalz D XII wire braced biplanes and the Fokker D VIII cantilever parasol monoplane. All these aircraft saw front line service with the *Jagdstaffeln* and possessed varying degrees of merit, but none were as popular with the pilots or capable of such excellent all-round fighting ability as the fine Fokker D VII.

2. Parachutes

Following the successful use of Paulus type parachutes on observation balloons, attempts were made to use them from aircraft, but the problem of canopy stowage and the requirement that the canopy be taken clear of the aircraft when the pilot jumped introduced difficulties that prevented the use of the Paulus system from aeroplanes. The balloon observer's parachute was pulled out of its container by the falling observer and only when fully extended did a weak attachment at the apex of the canopy sever, allowing separation from the balloon. Such a method was only suitable for use from a reasonably stable platform. There was less possibility of entanglement with the aircraft or damage to the canopy during deployment from a rapidly moving object such as an out of control or burning aeroplane with the Heinecke parachute since the pilot and packed canopy fell free from the aircraft first. A static line then pulled the canopy from its pack, but the length of static line had to suit the type of aeroplane. Isolated examples of pilot type

Immediate readiness. Pilots of *Jasta* 10 sitting in front of their Fokker D VIIs, September 1918. Left to right: *Unteroffizier* Hennig, *Leutnant* Schibilsky, *Leutnant* Grassmann, *Leutnant* Heldmann (acting *Staffelführer*), *Offizierstellvertreter* Aue, *Leutnant* Kohlbach, *Unteroffizier* Klamt and *Leutnant* Bähren. All pilots are wearing Heinecke parachute harness.

parachutes were issued to fighter pilots during 1917 for experimental purposes although there are no records to indicate that any were actually used in action. Pilots were sceptical about parachutes and even when they were issued in number to *Jagdstaffeln* during April/May 1918 it was not until news of several successful descents were made known that pilots began to trust them and wear them on all front line flights. By the end of the war they were in widespread use, and in September 1918 a total of 130 parachute descents were made, many of which were by fighter pilots using the Heinecke equipment. There were some instances of harness failure and both official and unofficial modifications led to the use of strengthened harnesses late in 1918.

3. Phosphorous Ammunition

The fearful wounds and agonizing deaths that some German airmen suffered after being hit by British phosphorous ammunition during 1916 caused pilots and observers to make an appeal via *Stofl* 6 (*Hptm.* Stempel) to the *Feldflugchef*. It was to the effect that unless a similar type of ammunition could be made available for their use fairly rapidly, an official communication should be sent to the British clearly stating that aviators who used this ammunition and became prisoners of war could not be guaranteed protection but would be shot out of hand. Experiments with German phosphorous ammunition began in November. During February 1917 a copy of the British phosphorous ammunition had been produced (Phosphor F) and was 100 per cent effective at a range of 300 metres against balloons; 250,000 rounds were ordered. Given the official designation of *Ph-Munition* on 15 March 1917, this ammunition could ignite a balloon at a range of 400 metres, and an aeroplane if the tank was hit from the same distance. Experiments continued to extend the useful range of this type of ammunition although it was known to be unstable and as a result had a very short storage life. Trouble with *Ph-Munition* reached a peak in July 1918 when it was used on the Fokker D VII. The ammunition boxes on this machine were close to the mass of the engine; aircraft at this time did not usually have a fireproof bulkhead aft of the engine, and the Fokker D VII was no exception. As a result, in hot weather the cartridges were subjected to high temperatures, a problem compounded by insufficient louvres to allow the cooling air passing through the radiator to escape quickly. Using phosphorous ammunition under these conditions when it was near the end of its safe storage life or possibly on extended life, aggravated by petrol contamination from nearby leaking fuel tanks, resulted in the self-ignition of rounds. Whether or not the exploding ammunition actually pierced the fuel tank was of little importance, as the result was the same—the aircraft burst into flames. This hazard was eventually alleviated by introducing additional cooling louvres to prevent the concentration of very warm air highly charged with petrol vapour in the forward fuselage and

by reducing the period of safe life of *Ph-Munition*. Additionally in very warm weather Fokker D VIIs were flown with certain cowling panels removed to increase ventilation of the area around the cartridge belt containers.

4. Fighter Aircraft Markings

A particular unit marking was the prerogative of the *Staffelführer* and once adopted it was communicated to the *Kofl* who ensured that the *Flak* units and the *Luftschutzoffiziere* at the front were aware of its nature. These personnel then used this knowledge when watching aerial activity. A study of unit markings shows that not only did the markings usually undergo a revision with a change of aircraft type and *Staffelführer*, but that they were also modified on occasion to prevent confusion with other units that sported similar markings. The style and nature of the personal emblems used by the pilots were also approved by the *Staffelführer*.

Their purpose was to provide individual identification in the air, and markings had to be of a size and colour that achieved this. Some *Staffelführer* were stricter than others in accepting a pilot's desired marking, and it is known that in some units individual emblems were forbidden and pilots had the engine cowlings or tail units of their aircraft painted in different colours to give positive identification, especially in the heat of a dogfight. The official views on camouflage finishes were given little thought in the *Jagdstaffeln* especially during the last nine months of the war. Since it was recognized that units would repaint plywood covered fuselages with their own markings, *Idflieg* relaxed the finishing paint schemes for this section of the airframe during aircraft acceptance inspection. Some units had the help of creative artists, who produced personal emblems of a high standard for the pilots. Other designs used for personal identification were copied directly from advertisements in the magazines of the day, or were related to some previous association with an army regiment, home town or family coat of arms. There is no doubt that some *Staffelführer* and pilots allowed the fascination of a pretty colour scheme or personal emblem to overrule its practicality as a means of identification. The quality of paint had steadily decreased as the war continued due to the shortage of raw materials, and occasionally it was the availability of a certain colour of paint or dope in quantity that decreed the shade adopted. The colours used in the application of both unit and personal markings tended to be unstable, and some were not even waterproof. Consequently after considerable service in the vicinity of mud, oil and petrol, they seldom resembled the pristine examples they had been at the time of application. It has been recorded that sometimes whitewash was used for lightening purposes and even boot polish was applied when nothing better was to hand to produce black. Allied to the practical problems of applying markings was the fact that attrition of D Category aircraft was extremely high. Accidents caused by weather, poor aerodromes, pilot error and mechanical failures as well as actual operational losses ensured that a fairly steady turnover of aircraft took place within most units. As a result, markings of a temporary nature usually did not cause undue problems, for by the time the paintwork started to crack and flake off, or lose its original colour, the machine had probably been written off or replaced.

Leutnant Neckel of *Jagdstaffel* **6** with his black and white striped Fokker D VII. The use of oblique striping was commonly thought to provide protection through optical illusion, and many pilots used variations of this theme, amongst them *Leutnant* **Ernst Udet** (*Jasta* **4**) and *Leutnant* **Kirschstein** (*Jasta* **6**).

APPENDIX III

Jagdstaffeln formed after 1 January 1917

Jagdstaffel	Date of Designation	Date of Formation	Jagdstaffel	Date of Designation	Date of Formation
26	14.12.16	18.1.17	60	11.1.18	24.1.18
27	5.2.17	5.2.17	61	11.1.18	24.1.18
28 (w)	14.12.16	21.1.17	62	16.1.18	25.1.18
29	28.12.16	12.2.17	63	16.1.18	26.1.18
30	14.12.16	21.1.17	64 (w)	23.1.18	4.2.18
31	14.12.16	5.2.17	65	23.1.18	4.1.18
32 (b)	14.12.16	22.2.17	66	27.1.18	5.2.18
33	14.12.16	1.3.17	67	27.1.18	5.2.18
34 (b)	20.2.17	20.2.17	68	1.2.18	10.2.18
35 (b)	14.12.16	1.3.17	69	1.2.18	10.2.18
36	11.1.17	21.2.17	70	6.2.18	18.2.18
37	10.1.17	10.1.17	71	6.2.18	17.2.18
38	30.6.17	30.6.17	72 (s)	11.2.18	20.2.18
39	30.6.17	10.8.17	73	11.2.18	20.2.18
40 (s)	30.6.17	15.8.17	74	16.2.18	25.2.18
41	18.6.17	5.8.17	75	16.2.18	25.2.18
42	6.12.17	18.12.17	76 (b)	15.10.17	15.10.17
43	6.12.17	18.12.17	77 (b)	25.11.17	25.11.17
44 (s)	11.12.17	23.12.17	78 (b)	15.12.17	15.12.17
45	11.12.17	23.12.17	79 (b)	28.1.18	28.1.18
46	11.12.17	25.12.17	80 (b)	15.2.18	16.2.18
47 (w)	16.12.17	26.12.17	81	15.6.17	15.6.17
48	16.12.17	1.1.18	82	29.10.18	Previously *Kest* 2
49	23.12.17	9.1.18	83	29.10.18	Previously *Kest* 3
50	23.12.17	5.1.18	84 (w)	29.10.18	Previously *Kest* 4a & 4b
51	27.12.17	9.1.18	85	29.10.18	Previously *Kest* 5
52	27.12.17	9.1.18	86	29.10.18	Previously *Kest* 6
53	27.12.17	7.1.18	87	29.10.18	Previously *Kest* 7
54 (s)	1.1.18	15.1.18	88	29.10.18	Previously *Kest* 8
55*	1.1.18	25.1.18	89	29.10.18	Previously *Kest* 9
56	1.1.18	12.1.18	90	29.10.18	Previously *Kest* 1a & 1b
57	6.1.18	19.1.18			
58	6.1.18	20.1.18			
59	6.1.18	21.1.18			

On 4 July 1917, *Jagdstaffeln* 16, 23, 32, 34, and 35 were given Bavarian affiliations, and on 24 November 1917, *Jagdstaffeln* 21, 22, 24, and 40 were made Saxon formations. In the above listing b = Bavarian, s = Saxon, w = *Württemberger*.

* Became 1(F)

APPENDIX IV Single-seat fighter pilots awarded the *Pour le mérite*

Rank	Name	Final score	Last unit	Rank	Name	Final score	Last unit
Leutnant	Karl Allmenroeder	30	*Jasta* 11	Leutnant	Gustav Leffers	9	*Jasta* 1
Oberleutnant	Ernst Freiherr			Oberleutnant	Erich Loewenhardt	54	*Jasta* 10
	von Althaus	10	*Jasta* 10	Hauptmann	Bruno Loerzer	44	JG 3
Leutnant	Oliver Freiherr			Leutnant	Karl Menckhoff	39	*Jasta* 72
	von Beaulieu-			Leutnant	Max Ritter		
	Marconnay	26	*Jasta* 19		von Müller	38	*Jasta* 2
Leutnant	Paul Bäumer	43	*Jasta* 2*	Leutnant	Max Ritter		
Oberleutnant	Otto Bernert	28	*Jasta* 2		von Mulzer	10	F.Fl.
Oberleutnant	Hans Berr	10	*Jasta* 5				Abt 5b
Hauptmann	Rudolf Berthold	44	JG 2	Leutnant	Ulrich Neckel	30	*Jasta* 6
Leutnant	Walter Blume	28	*Jasta* 9	Leutnant	Theodor Osterkamp	31	Marine
Leutnant	Erwin Böhme	25	*Jasta* 2				*Jasta* 2
Hauptmann	Oswald Boelcke	40	*Jasta* 2	Leutnant	Otto Parschau	8	KG 1
Oberleutnant	Oskar Freiherr			Leutnant	Fritz Pütter	25	*Jasta* 68
	von Boenigk	27	JG 2	Oberleutnant	Lothar Freiherr		
Rittmeister	Carl Bolle	36	*Jasta* 2		von Richthofen	40	*Jasta* 11
Leutnant	Heinrich Bongartz	33	*Jasta* 36	Rittmeister	Manfred Freiherr		
Leutnant	Julius Buckler	35	*Jasta* 17		von Richthofen	80	JG 1
Hauptmann	Hans-Joachim Buddecke	13	*Jasta* 30	Oberleutnant	Fritz Ritter		
Leutnant	Franz Büchner	40	*Jasta* 13		von Röth	28	*Jasta* 16
Leutnant	Walter von Bülow	28	*Jasta* 2	Leutnant	Fritz Rumey	45	*Jasta* 5
Leutnant	Karl Degelow	30	*Jasta* 40	Oberleutnant	Gotthard Sachsenberg	31	Marine
Leutnant	Albert Dossenbach	15	*Jasta* 10				*Jasta* 1
Oberleutnant	Eduard Ritter			Leutnant	Karl Emil Schäfer	30	*Jasta* 28
	von Dostler	26	*Jasta* 6	Hauptmann	Eduard Ritter		
Leutnant	Wilhelm Frankl	17	*Jasta* 4		von Schleich	35	JG 4
Hauptmann	Hermann Göring	22	JG 1	Leutnant	Karl Thom	27	*Jasta* 21
Leutnant	Heinrich Gontermann	39	*Jasta* 15	Leutnant	Emil Thuy	32	*Jasta* 28
Oberleutnant	Robert Ritter			Hauptmann	Adolf Ritter		
	von Greim	26	*Jasta* 34		von Tutschek	27	JG 2
Leutnant	Walter Höhndorf	12	*Jasta* 14	Oberleutnant	Ernst Udet	62	*Jasta* 4
Oberleutnant	Josef Jacobs	41	*Jasta* 7	Leutnant	Josef Veltjens	35	*Jasta* 15
Oberleutnant	Max Immelmann	15	KEK III	Leutnant	Werner Voss	50	*Jasta* 10
Leutnant	Hans Kirschstein	27	*Jasta* 6	Hauptmann	Franz Walz	7	Fl.Abt.
Oberleutnant	Otto Kissenberth	20	*Jasta* 23				304(b)
Leutnant	Hans Klein	22	*Jasta* 10	Leutnant	Rudolf Windisch	22	*Jasta* 66
Leutnant	Otto Könnecke	35	*Jasta**5	Leutnant	Kurt Wintgens	20	*Jasta* 1
Leutnant	Heinrich Kroll	33	*Jasta* 24	Oberleutnant	Kurt Wolff	33	*Jasta* 11
Leutnant	Arthur Laumann	26	*Jasta* 10	Leutnant	Kurt Wüsthoff	27	*Jasta* 15

*Named *Jasta Boelcke* on 17 December 1916

Jagdstaffeln usually effected a change of aerodrome by moving the complete unit by rail. Fokker D VII and Pfalz D XII single-seaters of *Jasta* 35b are shown loaded on flat railway cars at Bouchain on 25 September 1918.

Opposite:
Six Siemens single-seaters (D III and D IV) of *Jasta* 12 on Giraumont aerodrome, September 1918. The D IV marked with the white flash was flown by *Leutnant* Greven.

Pilots of *Jasta* 15 in front of *Leutnant* von Hantelmann's Fokker D VII following his twentieth victory, Charmois aerodrome near Stenay, 9 October 1918. Left to right: *Vizefeldwebel* Klaudat, *Leutnant* Glöcklen, *Leutnant* von Ziegesar, *Leutnant* Veltjens (*Staffelführer*), *Leutnant* von Hantelmann, *Leutnant* Schäfer and *Vizefeldwebel* Weischer.

Jagdgruppe **6**, October 1918. Left to right: *Leutnant* **Raab** (*Adjutant Gruja* 6), *Leutnant* **Plauth** (Acting *Staffelführer, Jasta* 51), *Leutnant* **Jacobs** (*Staffelführer, Jasta* 7), *Hauptmann* **Milch** (*Gruja* 6), *Leutnant* **Degelow** (*Staffelführer, Jasta* 40), and *Leutnant* **von Dazur** (*Staffelführer, Jasta* 20). Note the late use of the Fokker Dr I: *Leutnant* Jacobs preferred the triplane to the D VII and flew one until the end of the war.

Finis! Six Fokker D VIIs of *Jagdgeschwader* **3 seen at Nivelles in December 1918, with personnel of Nos. 85 and 54 Squadrons RAF. The machine nearest the camera was that flown by** *Oberleutnant* **Bolle,** *Staffelführer* **of** *Jasta Boelcke.* **When handed over to the Allies after the Armistice, it bore a young mechanic's inscription to the effect that this machine had brought down forty British aeroplanes.**

APPENDIX V
Glossary of terms*

Amerikaprogramm	America programme
Balkenkreuz	Straight sided cross
-Bogohl	Bombing squadron of the High Command
Feldflugchef	Chief of field aviation
Flugzeugwerke	Aircraft factory
Führer der Jagdgruppe (Gruja)	Leader of a non-permanent grouping of *Jagdstaffeln*
Gruppenkommando	Group of Army Corps Headquarters
Jagdgeschwader	Permanent group of *Jagdstaffeln* with a strength of approx. 50 aircraft
Jagdgruppe	Non-permanent group of *Jagdstaffeln*
Jagdstaffelschule	Fighter school
Jasta Ober Ost	Fighter unit of Eastern Front
Jagdraüme	Army HQ designated fighting area
Leutnant zur See	Naval lieutenant
Marine-Feld-Jagdgeschwader	Naval land based group of *Jagdstaffeln*
Marine-Feld-Jagdstaffel	Naval land based fighter unit
Oberstleutnant	Lieutenant-Colonel
Obersten Heeresleitung (OHL)	Army High Command
Panzer-Munition	Armour piercing ammunition
Ph-Munition	Phosphorous ammunition
Ritter	Knight
Seefrontstaffel } *Seefrosta* }	Single-seater fighter unit for the defence of the Flanders coast

* Supplement to appendix III in *German Fighter Units 1914–May 1917*

Notes sur les planches en couleur

Page 25 : *Oberleutnant* pilote auparavant du 1st Leibhusaren. Il porte une casquette mollette avec ruban et tuyautage en ses couleurs précédentes de régiment, et la tunique d'hussard 'Attila' avec brandebourgs magnifiques mouchetées en noir. Ses pattes d'épaule tiennent sous-étoffe en couleur de régiment, une étoile d'or et l'insigne d'escadre-et-propulseur d'or de sa nouvelle arme. L'insigne du pilote pryssien et l'*Iron Cross* sont portés. Longues guêtres sont articles pour pilotes d'arme typique en dehors des règles.

Page 26 dessus : Albatros D V volé de *Ltn.* Franz Müller, *Jagdstaffel* 11, été 1917. Les hautes surfaces d'escadres tiennent un fini surpeindu en couleurs de lilas et vert foncé. L'usage général de lilas comme une couleur de camouflage sur hautes surfaces résulta de la consigne *Idflieg* du 12.4.17 que régla précisément que cette couleur seulement fut être utilisée avec vert foncé pour tels faits. La surface rouge montré sur le fuselage en avant devint standard sur appareils de *Jasta* 11 ; toutes entretoises et couvertures des roues furent aussi peintes en la même couleur et ce comporta le marquage de fraction.

Page 26 dessous : Pfalz D III 4011/17 volé de *Ltn.* Fritz Höhn, *Jagdstaffel* 21, hiver 1917–1918. La raie noire et blanche d'ensemble encerclement le fuselage immédiatement en arrière de la carlingue est le marquage de fraction. Les marquages personnels de Höhn sont extraordinairement élaborés et en plus de la 'H' noire sur la carlingue y comportent raies noires en avant de la carlingue avec marquages rouges à l'arrière sur fuselage à l'arrière et sur l'empennage. Une habitude peu habituelle de *Jasta* 21 fut l'allocation de petits numéros individuels sur ses avions et cet appareil porte un tel numéro (10) au-dessous de son numéro de série sur le fuselage.

Page 27 : Fokker Dr I 413/17 volé de *Ltn.* Carl Bolle, *Staffelführer*, *Jagdstaffel Boelcke*, sur la fin de printemps/au début d'été 1918. Le fuselage à l'arrière noir et blanc, le stabilisateur et les gouvernails d'altitude, et le capotage noir de moteur avec panneau blanc en avant comportent le marquage de fraction. Le propre marquage de Bolle se compose de raies multicolores sur le fuselage, la large raie jaune représentant la couleur d'un son régiment précédent, Kürassier Regiment von Seydlitz No. 7. Fini normal pour ce type d'appareil fut pour toutes les surfaces d'en haut en de côtés être rayées en couleur verte/brune.

Pages 28–29 : Fokker D VII construit de Ostdeutsche Albatros-Werke (OAW). Volé de *Ltn.* Franz Büchner, *Staffelführer Jasta* 13, été/ automne 1918. Büchner fut de la Saxe et il utilisa les couleurs saxonnes de vert et blanc sur la raie à carreaux sur le fuselage, et vert comme la couleur de fond pour ses insignes de la tête de 'loup-garou' lesquels furent ses marquages personnels. Le fuselage, le stabilisateur et les gouvernails d'altitude surpeindu bleu foncé furent un marquage d'ordre introduit de *Hauptmann* Berthold, le *Kommandeur* de *Jagdgeschwader* 2 duquel *Jasta* 13 fut une fraction constituante.

Page 30 : Albatros D Va volé de *Ltn.* Ernst Udet. *Staffelführer, Jasta* 27, hiver 1917–1918. Le marquage de fraction fut le stabilisateur et les gouvernails d'altitude obliquement rayés en noir et blanc et quand Udet devint *Staffelführer* il introduit le marquage additionnel de carlingue noire sur fuselage, dérive, gouvernail de direction, toutes entretoises et couverture de roues. Pilotes de la fraction utilisèrent symboles sur le fuselage ordinairement en blanc, et grands numéros (1–14) sur les deux côtés du nez et sous les plus bas escadres pour identification personnelle. Udet porta le monogramme 'LO', que fut une abréviation du nom de sa fiancée, sur le fuselage et au lieu d'un numéro il utilisa chevrons blancs sur les deux côtés du nez.

Page 31 dessus : (A) Tête de démon ricanante qui fut un marquage personnel sur Albatros D III construit de OAW porté de *Vzfw.* Boldt, *Jasta* 31. En plus de ce marquage, Boldt montra courtes raies blanches autour de fuselage à l'arrière de la croix sur fuselage. (B) Écusson de la ville de Kiel utilisé de *Ltn.* Leptien comme un marquage personnel sur Albatros D Va de *Jasta* 63. Ceci fut appliqué au fuselage de contre-plaqué verni que fut décoré du marquage de fraction de grands diamants noirs. (C) Devise de roue extrait de l'écusson de famille et utilisé comme un marquage personnel sur Fokker DR I par *Ltn.* Hasso von Wedel de *Jasta* 14. La raie horizontale noire et blanche visible sur les deux côtés de ce marquage est l'identification de fraction et elle s'étendit du nez à l'empennage. (D) Marquage de cigogne porté sur Fokker D VII par *Uffz.* Piel de *Jasta* 13 comme un marquage personnel. Cet appareil tint un nez vert et un fuselage et un empennage surpeindu en bleu similaire à ceux illustrés dans le tableau à cinq perspectives. La division de couleur fut verticale 2ft. en avant de la carlingue. (E) Appareils Fokker D VII de *Jasta*

18 tinrent toutes surfaces d'en haut et de côtés en avant de la division verticale illustrée surpeindus en vermillon clair, le fuselage à l'arrière et l'empennage surpeindus en blanc et il portèrent de plus un corbeau noir (*der Rabe*) dans la situation illustrée pour indiquer le nom du *Staffelführer, Ltn.* August Raben. Insignes différents sur côtés de fuselage et décorations assorties de stabilisateur/gouvernail d'altitude garantirent identification individuelle de pilote. Le motif de quatre poussins illustré fut utilisé de *Ltn.* Günther von Büren. (F) Insigne de casque ailé fondé sur mythologie Valkyrie utilisé comme un marquage personnel de *Oblt.* Hermann Dahlmann, Capitaine adjutant major de *Jagdgeschwader* 3. Son Fokker D VII actionné par moteur BMW tint un nez peindu noir, et fuselage, stabilisateur et gouvernails d'altitude rayés en raies noires et blanches du marquage de fraction de *Jasta* 26.

Page 31 dessous : *Jagdstaffeln* tinrent un effectif de deux remorques pour le transport de charges encombrantes y comris avions. L'exemple illustré fut sur les contrôles de *Jasta* 19 pendant automne 1917 et il est chargé avec Albatros D V 2031/17.

Page 32 gauche : Pilote mis en vêtements complets d'aviateur avec harnais de parachute Heinecke, 1918. La distribution spéciale de Fliegerhosen sont portés avec un dolman de cuir personellement acheté, casque et lunettes protectrices. L'harnais est renforcé avec cuir et il tient extralarges courroies pour les jambes ; quelques premiers harnais faillirent. Le pilote fut assis sur le parachute et la ligne statique fut liée d'une manière permanente avec l'avion.

Page 32 droit : *Leutnant* pilote, ex-12th Ulans mis en British dolman d'aviateur capturé—un article populaire—avec col de fourrure ajouté. Ruban de casquette et tuyautage en couleur de bleut. Bandes-molletières et bottines remplacèrent souvent bottes à revers pour usage ordinaire.

Farbtafeln

Seite 25 : Oberleutnant Pilot, ehemals 1. Leibhusaren. Er trägt eine weiche Schirmmütze mit Band und Paspel seiner alten Regimentsfarben, den Husaren 'Attila' Waffenrock mit reichlich schwarzgeflecktem Schnürbesatz. Seine Achselklappen sind in den Regimentsfarben unterlegt, goldener Rangpaspel und das goldene Flügel und Propeller Abzeichen sind Zeichen seines neuen Dienstes. Das preussische Pilotenabzeichen und das Eiserne Kreuz werden getragen. Lange Gamaschen sind typische lässige Dienstbekleidung.

Seite 26 oben : Albatros D V von Ltn. Franz Müller, Jagdstaffel 11, geflogen ; Sommer 1917. Die oberen Seiten der Tragflächen sind in lila- und grüngestrichener Ausführung. Die weitverbreitete Verwendung von Lila als Oberflächen-Tarnfarbe folgte der Idflieg (Inspektion der Fliegertruppen) Verordnung vom 12.4.17, welche ausdrücklich festlegte, dass nur diese Farbe im Zusammenhang mit Dunkelgrün für diese Zwecke verwandt werde. Der rote Flächenraum des vorderen Rumpfes wurde die Norm an Maschinen in Jasta 11 ; alle Streben und Radkappen waren in der gleichen Farbe gestrichen und waren somit Markierung der Einheit.

Seite 26 unten : Pfalz D III 4011/17 von Ltn. Fritz Höhn, Jagdstaffel 21, geflogen ; Winter 1917/18. Das schwarz-weisse Band, welches den Rumpf direkt hinter dem Führersitz umringt, ist die Markierung der Einheit. Höhns persönliche Markierungen sind ungewöhnlich ausführlich ; ausser dem schwarzen 'H' schloss es schwarze Streifen vor der Kanzel und rote Markierungen am hinteren Rumpf und Leitwerk ein. Ein ungewöhnlicher Brauch in der Jagdstaffel 21 war die Verteilung von kleinen individuellen Nummern an den Flugzeugen. Diese Maschine hier trägt eine solche Nummer (10) unter der Seriennummer auf dem Rumpf.

Seite 27 : Fokker Dr I 413/17, von Ltn. Carl Bolle, Staffelführer der Jagdstaffel Boelcke, spätes Frühjahr/früher Sommer 1918, geflogen. Der schwarz-weisse hintere Rumpf, Schwanzfläche und Höhensteuer, und die schwarze Motorenhaube mit weisser Front umfasste die Markierung der Einheit. Bolles eigene Markierungen bestanden aus mehrfarbigen Bändern um den Rumpf ; das breite gelbe Band vertritt die Farbe seines alten Regimentes, dem Kürassier Regiment von Seydlitz Nr. 7. Standardausführung für diesen Maschinentyp war, dass alle Ober-und

Seitenflächen grün/braungestrichelt waren. Die unteren Flächen waren hellblau.

Seiten 28–29: Fokker D VII von Ostdeutsche Albatros-Werke (OAW) gebaut, geflogen von Ltn. Franz Büchner, Staffelführer Jasta 13, Sommer/Herbst 1918. Büchner kam aus Sachsen und benutzte die Landesfarben Grün und Weiss als kariertes Band um den Rumpf und Grün als Hintergrund für sein Werwolfkopf-Abzeichen als persönliche Markierung. Der Rumpf, Schwanzfläche und Höhensteuer in Blau überstrichen war eine Formationsmarkierung; eingeführt von Hauptmann Berthold, Kommandeur des Jagdgeschwader 2, von welchem Jagdstaffel 13 ein Bestandteil war. Einheitsmarkierung (Jasta 13) besteht aus grüner Nase mit weissem Streifen.

Seite 30: Albatros D Va gelfogen von Ltn. Ernst Udet, Staffelführer Jasta 37, Winter 1917/18. Die Markierung der Einheit waren die schrägen schwarzweissgestreiften Schwanzflächen und Höhensteuer. Als Udet Staffelführer wurde, fügte er den schwarzüberstrichenen Rumpf, Kielflosse, Seitensteuer, alle Streben und Radkappen hinzu. Piloten der Einheit gebrauchten Symbole am Rumpf—gewöhnlich in Weiss—und grosse Nummern (1–14) auf beiden Seiten der Nase und unter den unteren Tragflächen als persönliche Identifizierung. Udet führte das Monogramm 'LO'—kurz für Lola—dem Namen seiner Verlobten. Anstelle einer Nummer hatte er einen weissen Winkel auf beiden Seiten der Nase.

Seite 31 oben: (A) Grinsender Teufelskopf, persönliche Markierung auf einem OAW gebauten Albatros D III Vzfw. Boldt, Jasta 31. Ausserdem zeigte Boldtes Markierung kurze weisse Balken um den Rumpf hinter dem Kreuz. (B) Wappenschild der Stadt Kiel von Ltn. Leptien als persönliche Markierung auf Albatros D Va in Jasta 63 benutzt. Es wurde auf einen lackierten Sperrholzrumpf aufgetragen, welcher von Nase bis Schwanz mit der Einheitsmarkierung von grossen schwarzen Rauten dekoriert war. (C) Ein Ostpreussisches Richtrad, dem Familienwappen entnommen, wurde von Ltn. Hasso von Wedel als persönliche Abzeichen am Fokker Dr I in Jagdstaffel 14 benutzt. Der horizontale schwarz-weisse Streifen, der sich auf beiden Seiten der Nase zum Schwanz hinzieht, ist die Identifizierung der Einheit. (D) Das Zeichen eines Storches wurde von Uffz. Piel, Jagdstaffel 13, auf Fokker D VII als persönliche Markierung geflogen. Diese Maschine hatte eine grüne Nase und einen blauüberstrichenen Rumpf und Leitwerk, wie man auf der Vierseiten-Ansicht erkennen kann. Die Miniatur-Kokarden sind Stoffstücke über Einschusslöchern, die gewöhnlich mit dem Datum der Einschüsse versehen wurden. (E) Fokker D VII Maschinen der Jasta 18 hatten alle oberen und seitlichen Flächen vor der senkrechten Unterteilung in einem leuchtenden Scharlachrot überstrichen; der hintere Rumpf und Leitwerk waren in Weiss überstrichen. Ausserdem trugen sie einen schwarzen Raben an der gezeigten Stelle, um den Namen des Staffelführers—Ltn. August Raben—zu kennzeichnen. Unterschiedliche Abzeichen an den Rumpfseiten und verschiedene Schwanzflächen/Höhensteuerverzierungen leisteten Gewähr für individuelle Pilotenidentifizierung. Das gezeigte 'Vier Hühner'—Motiv wurde von Ltn. Günther von Büren benutzt. (F) Das 'Geflügelte Helm'—Zeichen—aus der skandinavischen Mythologie-wurde von Oberleutnant Hermann Dahlmann (Adjutant des JG 3) geflogen. Sein Fokker D VII (BMW Motoren) hatte eine schwarzgestrichene Nase. Rumpf, Schwanzflächen und Höhensteuer waren mit schwarzweissgestreiften Balken in der einheitlichen Markierung von Jasta 26.

Seite 31 unten: Jagdstaffeln hatten eine Stärke von zwei Anhängern für den Transport von Sperrgut einschliesslich Flugzeugen. Das gezeigte Beispiel stammt von Jasta 19 während des Herbstes 1917; er ist mit Albatros D V 2031/17 beladen.

Seite 32 links: Pilot in voller Fliegerausrüstung mit Heinecke-Gurtwerk 1918. Die Fliegerhosen sind eine Sonderausgabe, sie werden mit privatlich erworbenen Ledermantel, Helm und Schutzbrille getragen. Das Gurtwerk ist mit Leder verstärkt und hat besonders breite Beinriemen; einige der früheren Gurtwerke scheiterten. Der Pilot sass auf dem Fallschirm, welcher sich beim Absprung durch die statische Schnur öffnete, die am Flugzeug befestigt war.

Seite 32 rechts: Leutnant Pilot, ehemals 12. Ulanen, mit britischem Fliegermantel—ein beliebtes Stück—mit hinzugefügtem Pelzkragen. Mützenband und Paspel in Kornblumenblau und Weiss stammen aus dem alten Regiment. Die silbernen Kord-Achselklappen sind mit dem Kornblumenblau des Regimentsbesatzes unterlegt. Wickelgamaschen und hohe Schuhe wurden oft durch Stulpenstiefel als Alltagskleidung ersetzt.

AIRWAR SERIES

First 20 titles:

1 RAF Fighter Units, Europe, 1939–42

2 USAAF Heavy Bomber Units, ETO & MTO, 1942–45

3 Spanish Civil War Air Forces

4 Luftwaffe Ground Attack Units, 1939–45

5 RAF Bomber Units, 1939–42

6 Luftwaffe Fighter Units, Europe, 1939–41

7 USAAF Medium Bomber Units, ETO & MTO, 1942–45

8 USAAF Fighter Units, Europe, 1942–45

9 Luftwaffe Night Fighter Units, 1939–45

10 RAF Fighter Units, Europe, April 1942–45

11 Luftwaffe Fighter Units, Russia, 1941–45

12 USAAF Fighter Units, MTO, 1942–45

13 German Fighter Units, 1914–May 1917

14 British Fighter Units, Western Front, 1914–16

15 Luftwaffe Bomber Units, 1939–41

16 US Navy Carrier Air Groups, Pacific, 1941–45

17 German Fighter Units, June 1917–1918

18 British Fighter Units, Western Front, 1917–18

19 RAF Bomber Units, July 1942–1945

20 Luftwaffe Fighter Units, Mediterranean, 1941–44

Planned titles:

Japanese Carrier Air Groups, 1941–45

USAAF Bomber Units, Pacific, 1941–45

RAF Combat Units, SEAC, 1941–45

Luftwaffe Fighter Units, Europe, 1942–45